Rise and Fall

The Construction and Destruction of a Baseball Dynasty

John Bartolick

© 2008 by John Bartolick
Garwood, New Jersey USA
bartolick@comcast.net
All rights reserved

ISBN 978-0-578-01632-0

Written in memory of my mother, who ignited my passion for the game of baseball.

Contents

The End	2
The Last Of The Old-Fashioned Dynasties	4
The $100,000 Infield - Prelude to Déjà Vu	9
Fate	16
The Arbiter	17
The Johnson Years	23
The New Owner	28
The Seeds of a Dynasty	34
The Basement	38
Recruiting	43
Rule IV	50
Building and Rebuilding	59
The Setback	67
Goodbye Kansas City, Hello Oakland	75
Perfection On The Road To Respectability	80
Priming the Engine	89
Dress Rehearsal	103
The Mustache Gang	113
The Over-the-Hill Gang	128
The Big Red Machine and the Great World Series of 1972	143
The World Takes Notice	154
Turmoil	156
Battling the Upstarts -The Second Great World Series	173
Hardball	185
Help Wanted	187
Threepeat – Once More in '74	196
Ruthless Efficiency	206
First Exit	216
Hollow Victory	222
The Beginning of the End	235
Break Up the A's	239
Exodus	247
After the Storm	251
For Sale	255
What If?	258
Bibliography	264
Index	266

Acknowledgements

I am extremely grateful to the research staff of the A. Bartlett Giamatti Research Center at the National Baseball Hall of Fame in Cooperstown, New York for the assistance that they provided during my research for this book. I hope they realize that they have one of the greatest jobs in the world, and they do it very well. I am also appreciative of the support that I received from the photo archivists at Arizona State University and the Associated Press. Despite that fact that I am a completely unknown, self-publishing author, everyone that I have worked with has treated me with the utmost respect and commitment.

This book would also not have been possible without the support and assistance of my wife, Helen, and the friends too numerous to mention that have inspired me and in some cases pushed me to bring the idea for this book to fruition.

My final and most sincere thanks goes out to anyone and everyone that takes the time to read this story. I hope that I have rewarded your choice to pick up this book by telling the story well and accurately and that I have succeeded in bringing the 1970's Oakland Athletics to life in an interesting way.

Preface

I am not and have never been a fan of the Oakland Athletics, particularly the Oakland Athletics of the 1970's. I daresay that I was like most baseball fans throughout America in the 70's – for some reason the Athletics rubbed me the wrong way. Maybe it was their habit of thumbing their collective noses at the tradition-rich institution of baseball, maybe it was their bizarre uniforms, maybe it was the flamboyance and cockiness of their players, or maybe it was their owner, a man that every baseball fan loved to hate. It was probably all of the above, compounded by the fact that they had a very annoying habit of winning; dominating the competition at a time when the team I did root for, the New York Yankees, were going through one of the roughest periods of their storied history. Even my favorite player of the era, Cincinnati Reds' pitcher Don Gullett, fell victim to the Athletics and their success in the 1972 World Series. But I must admit that the passage of the years has diminished the hard feelings that I harbored for the Athletics, replacing them with a grudging admiration. I can now appreciate the Athletics for their slow, laborious climb from the basement to the top of their profession, and for the very special place that they hold in the history of baseball.

This book is really a story about the climb of a baseball team from obscurity to success beyond their wildest imaginations, a record of success rarely matched in the long history of the sport. I am not a professional baseball research specialist – I am a baseball fan, and I will attempt to tell the story from that perspective. The intended audience is likewise not the hard-core researcher, seeking a source of encyclopedic information about the subject – there are volumes of that type of information already available on this subject, more thorough than I could ever hope to compile. The intended audience is people like myself – people that are either passionate about the game of baseball and / or who just love a great baseball story. I don't recall when the idea to tell this story came to me, but at some point I realized that the story of the 1970's dynasty of the Oakland Athletics combines two great personal passions – the history of baseball and the art of building a great team. It is this latter element that makes the 1970's Athletics such a compelling subject. Despite the greatness of many of the individual players that wore the Athletic uniform during their dominance of the American League western division from 1971-1975, it was they way they interacted as a unit that illustrated a near perfect balance of speed, power, defense and pitching. Furthermore, it was the way that unit was painstakingly built from the ground up, piece-by-piece, that makes the final product so impressive. The team's sudden fall from grace serves as the perfect, ironic capstone for their story.

Much has been made of the off-field antics of the collection of characters that comprised the championship era Oakland Athletics. Often overshadowing their accomplishments on the field, the interpersonal dynamics of the parties could and indeed have filled volumes of written work. While no book on these Athletic teams would be complete without some reference to the utter turmoil that prevailed in the Oakland front offices and clubhouse, this element of the tale will not be emphasized in this book. Nor will the statistical details of the individual contributors be highlighted, impressive though they are. No baseball book would be complete without some statistical background, but every attempt will be made to limit such references to the minimum necessary to tell the story. For it is that story, the success on the field and the steps that led to that success, that is the centerpiece and that marks this series of Athletic teams as one of the most noteworthy in the annals of baseball history. The focus of this book will therefore be on how this series of championships came to be, as well as how, in the words of General George C. Patton, all glory is fleeting.

Setting the Stage

The End

It had taken slightly over two hours, a mere blink of an eye by later standards. For the Los Angeles Dodgers, the season was on the line. After a long, difficult regular-season battle against the powerful Cincinnati Reds and a challenging three-games-to-one League Championship victory against the equally dangerous Pittsburgh Pirates, the Dodgers had stood their ground against the defending World Champion Oakland Athletics. But thus far the Athletics had proven to be too much for the National League champs, taking three of the first four games of the 1974 World Series. The teams were well-matched, with three of the first four games decided by a single run and the fifth game tied into the bottom of the seventh when a Joe Rudi home run put the Athletics in the lead by a run. Now it was the bottom of the ninth, and the Dodgers were pulling out all of the stops to extend the game, the series, and their season just a little longer. With Rollie Fingers, a future Hall of Famer and one of the game's top relief pitchers, on the mound it would not be easy. Ron Cey and pinch hitter Willie Crawford were retired easily. The Dodgers' hopes rested on pinch hitter Von Joshua, a .234 hitter in the regular season. Joshua softly grounded a pitch to Fingers, who threw to first baseman Gene Tenace to complete the victory. The Athletics were once again the World Champions.

And so began a ritual that was repeated nine times over the last three seasons – the Athletics celebrated a championship. Three divisional titles, three American League Championships, three World Championships. They were truly at the top of their game and had earned a place among the greatest teams of all time. It was a truly remarkable

The End

journey for a team that had started out at the very bottom, a team that was painstakingly built piece-by-piece, slowly rising first to mediocrity, then respectability, then to the top of their division, then to the top of the world. Despite their storybook rise, they had attracted many more critics and people that despised them than they did fans and followers. But their players were still in their prime and the franchise had every right to expect that their dominance of the baseball world would continue unabated for many more years, despite the atmosphere of animosity that seemed to hang over the franchise like a cloud. Yet on that October evening in 1974, few could have predicted that it would all come apart as the talent that they had so carefully assembled would evaporate as if it had never existed; a team that took eleven years to build virtually from the ground up would completely disintegrate in just two.

And when it was all over, baseball would never be the same.

The Last Of The Old-Fashioned Dynasties

The Oakland Athletics of 1971-1975 were the last dynasty of an era that ended with a sea change in the way Major League Baseball teams were constructed.

Dynasties, in the traditional sense, span a long period of time, often generations. In the ever-changing landscape of professional baseball, such a standard is incredibly difficult to meet. If the term dynasty were to be applied conservatively, only the New York Yankees franchise would come close to qualifying. More appropriately, the term is generally applied to teams that sustain leadership within their league structure for a multiple-year period. The Oakland Athletics of 1971-1975 clearly fall into this category. Their five-year run atop the American League western division, punctuated by three consecutive World Championships from 1972-1974, is emblematic of the way in which this collection of teams dominated the competition during this period. Considering the fact that the team finished second in the division in each of the two seasons preceding this run and again the season after (narrowly missing a sixth consecutive divisional title by a mere two-and-a half games in 1976), the Oakland Athletics clearly established a record of success that earns them the recognition as a dynasty.

There were other excellent teams in both leagues during this period. The Minnesota Twins had won consecutive divisional titles just prior to the run of championships by the Athletics, just a few seasons after Minnesota won the 1965 American League Championship. But as solid as the Twins were, they were unable to progress beyond the League

The Last Of The Old-Fashioned Dynasties

Championship Series, in which they were twice swept. Their divisional series adversary both times was the great Baltimore Orioles team of the era. The Orioles easily won the American League Championship from 1969-1971 and again in 1973 and 1974. Unfortunately, they were only able to capture a World Series crown once during that period and they were defeated by the Athletics in two of the three League Championship series in which they met. Likewise, the National League's Cincinnati Reds were the champions of the National League western division for five out of seven years in 1970, 1972-1973, and 1975-1976. They made it to the World Series in four of those five championship seasons, but were only able to achieve victories in the final two World Series of that sequence. The inability of those great Baltimore and Cincinnati teams to sustain uninterrupted leadership at the top of their division or to more consistently translate regular-season success into a post-season triumph leave them just a notch below the Oakland Athletics of that same period.

None of the Athletic teams from the 1971-1975 period stands alone as an example of a truly great ballclub. Their best winning percentages were .627 in 1971 and .605 in 1975 – two years in which they did NOT reach the World Series. Their biggest margin of divisional victory during their three-year World Championship run was a mere six games. They did not possess a stockpile of talent on their bench or in their minor league system. They were constantly on the prowl for role players to fill what seemed to be a never-ending series of gaps on their roster. They built a solid core of stars that they surrounded with a rotating group of castoffs. Rather than blowing away the opposition, they practically patented the one-run victory. They always seemed to be

Rise and Fall

living on the brink of disaster. Yet they were the most feared franchise of their era. Their opponents knew from the first drill of spring training to the final out of the World Series that the Athletics were a formidable foe that always seemed to find a way to win. And their trademark brashness and cockiness demonstrated that the Athletics understood this as well.

From an historical perspective, the Athletics of the 70's were not the greatest dynasty in the history of the game of professional baseball. They may not even be in the top ten. They may not have even been the greatest collective team in A's franchise history; a designation that may be better bestowed upon Connie Mack's great Philadelphia Athletic teams of 1910-1914 and 1929-1933. They were obviously not the first dynasty in baseball history, nor were they the last – fans of the Atlanta Braves and the New York Yankees can accurately point to the dominance of their ball clubs within their divisions, and the Yankees three year run of World Championships from 1998-2000 matched the three consecutive championships earned by the Athletics. They were not the first dynasty built from the ground up from of the ashes of a perennial losing franchise. They were not the only dynasty to face a sudden and total collapse immediately after their time at the top. The Athletics were, however, the very last of a now extinct breed – a dynasty painstakingly built virtually from scratch without the benefit of the free agency system that changed the landscape of professional baseball. After the Athletics of the 1970's, teams endowed with the requisite financial resources could either utilize the available pool of free agents to build and continuously restock their rosters, or exploit the disrupting effect of free agency to

The Last Of The Old-Fashioned Dynasties

arrange trades to liberate high-priced talent that could not be sustained by their current clubs. As an example, when the New York Yankees of the turn of the 21st Century needed a player, they simply tapped into owner George Steinbrenner's endless coffers of cash, rubbed their magic lamp, and out would pop a genie that looked a lot like Alex Rodriguez, Wade Boggs, Jason Giambi, or whatever other specific player they wanted. This practice was not without risk and by no means did it guarantee a championship for any team. It did, however, create a continuously changing competitive landscape, making a sustained run at the top of a division even more difficult for teams that lacked the financial assets to continuously restock their talent pool. In addition, it clearly offered teams that were well endowed with cash the distinct advantage over teams that could not compete in the free agent market or retain their top talent. Teams like Steinbrenner's Yankees were liberated to the point that they could engage in overkill tactics to populate their rosters with stars at virtually every position, supported by the highest quality bench that money could by. This approach was perfected by the Yankees themselves as they won the 1977 World Championship in the very first year of the free agent era and the year that the A's dynasty self-destructed.

The story of the Athletics' 1971-1975 dynasty and the subsequent collapse is heavy with irony. The story virtually mirrors not one but two previous chapters in the history of the franchise. The amateur free agent draft that helped shape the team's roster was at least

Rise and Fall

in part derived from the excesses of the A's amateur bonus policies of the 1960's. And the harbinger of the birth of baseball free agency was twice played out when two marquee Athletic players gained free agency status in "one-off" episodes that served as a predictor and a warning of a world in which established players could sell their services to the highest bidder. Indeed, the very free agency system that in the end led to the end of the Athletics' dynasty was largely fueled by the stark break with the traditions of the game's past, a break borne in large part from seeds sown by the A's iconoclastic ownership. In the end, the dynasty of the Athletics was ended by changes that the team itself had catalyzed.

The $100,000 Infield - Prelude to Déjà Vu

The original Athletics of Philadelphia were the very first dynasty of the American League. During the ten-year period from 1905-1914, the Athletics won the American League Championship five times and captured four World Series titles. The only American League team to approach the heroics of the Athletics during that era was the Detroit Tigers, winners of three consecutive American League titles from 1907-1909. But unlike the Athletics, those early Tiger teams were unable to translate regular-season success into a World Championship, losing the World Series in each of those years. So it was the Athletics that set the early standard for excellence in the American League. Under the leadership of legendary owner / manager Connie Mack, the Athletics featured a balance of hitting, pitching, and defense that earned the club a place among the greatest teams in baseball history.

The highlight of the Athletics' decade-long run was the period from 1910-1914 when the team finished in first place four times. In those four seasons they averaged a winning percentage of .646 and finished an average of almost eleven games ahead of their next closest competitor in the eight-team league. Hall of Famers Chief Bender and Eddie Plank, a devastating righty / letfy combination, anchored Mack's pitching staff. Though less famous than Bender and Plank, Jack Coombs provided additional depth for the pitching staff. One of the truly dominant pitchers of his era, Coombs won an average of almost 27 games a year from 1910-1912 before being sidelined by typhoid fever.

Rise and Fall

The disease robbed him of most of his physical ability and virtually ended his career with the Athletics.

As dominant as Mack's pitching staff was, the champion Athletic teams of the era prior to the First World War are typically remembered for their infield. Dubbed "The $100,000 Infield" as a tribute to their value, the core of the unit assembled in 1909 when second baseman Eddie Collins, shortstop Jack Barry, and third baseman Frank Baker assumed the role of starters in their respective positions. The trio was joined on a full-time basis by first baseman John P. "Stuffy" McInnis in 1911 and the $100,000 infield was complete. Baker earned the moniker "Home Run Baker", a reflection of the baseball public's affinity for the long ball, by leading the American League with a whopping eleven home runs in 1911 and by following that up with two more round-trippers in the 1911 World Series against John McGraw's New York Giants. Baker led the American League in home runs each year from 1911-1914, peaking at 12 home runs in 1913, adding another World Series homer in 1913. Though unimpressive by later standards, Baker's home run heroics caught the imagination of dead-ball era baseball fans and eventually earned him a place in the Baseball Hall of Fame. Collins likewise earned enshrinement in the Hall on the basis of the 3,315 regular-season hits he collected and his .328 batting average in six World Series appearances. Collins was one of the American League's first superstars and a true franchise player. Though not a Hall of Famer, McInnis compiled a .307 lifetime batting average and set an early standard for defensive excellence at first base.

The $100,000 Infield - Prelude to Déjà Vu

Yes, the years of 1910-1914 were good to the Athletics. By 1914 Mack's infielders were in their prime at an average age of only 26, and although Coombs was ill and Bender and Plank were now in their thirties, the 1914 team was fortunate to have two exciting future pitching stars in Bob Shawkey and Hall of Famer Herb Pennock. But things were about to change and that change would be rapid and disastrous for the team. When Mack's infield reached notoriety after their first World Championship together, it was said that Mack "wouldn't take $100,000 for them". The bitter irony of that statement would soon be apparent to Philadelphia fans.

The seeds of the destruction of the Athletics' first dynasty were sown even prior to the 1914 season. In the decades prior to 1914, Major League Baseball players were bound to their teams by baseball's infamous "reserve clause". The reserve clause put virtually all of the power in the player / owner relationship firmly in the hands of the owners. By binding a player to the team that owned their "reserve", this pact had the obvious impact of limiting the contractual bargaining position of the individual players by restricting their options to two – accept the contracts offered by the ownership or refrain from playing professional baseball. It would be fifty years before players banded together in an effective collective bargaining unit, and another decade beyond that before the reserve clause would be rewritten. But for a two-year period beginning in 1914 the dynamic changed, and the impact on Mack's Athletics would be nothing short of catastrophic.

Rise and Fall

Prior to the 1914 season, a group of businessmen challenged the monopolistic dominance of the existing Major League Baseball leagues. With their support, a new eight-team major league christened the Federal League was launched. Often competing in cities with existing American or National League franchises, the Federal League declared war on the existing baseball leagues by refusing to recognize the existing reserve structure between current professional players and their teams and by raising the roof on salaries. As a result, the Federal League lured a number of established players to the new franchises by outbidding their current clubs for their services. This took an immediate toll on the rosters of the American and National League teams. In order to retain their players, owners began to increase player salaries, particularly those for the stars that were the primary targets of Federal League clubs seeking to establish themselves as legitimate baseball teams. The ensuing salary war with the upstart league resulted in significant upward adjustments of the salary structure. The Athletics, laden as they were with stars, were particularly vulnerable to this change in the status quo. The prospect and later the reality of dealing with a significantly rising cost of operation due to rising salaries caused great concern for Mack, coming as it did without a corresponding increase in revenues. Unable to drive his income any higher, Mack did what many business people in his position would do – he cut his costs. Since he could not profitably compensate his stable of stars in the economic climate of the Federal League years, Mack concluded that his only option was to sell his top players to reduce his operating costs and generate short-term income. This tactic, along with the defection of several Athletic players to the Federal League, changed the makeup of Mack's team almost overnight.

The $100,000 Infield - Prelude to Déjà Vu

The trouble started prior to the 1914 season when three Athletics, including 14-game winner Byron Houck, jumped from the Athletics to the new league. This turned out to be simply the tip of the iceberg. In the December following the 1914 season, Hall of Fame pitchers Bender and Plank jumped to the new league. It is important to remember that when a player jumped to the new league the former team received no compensation. Seeing the writing on the wall, Mack started taking proactive steps to cut his losses and protect his investment in the club as best he could. Within a week of the defection of Bender and Plank, Mack took the extraordinary step of selling Eddie Collins, the anchor of his previously untouchable $100,000 infield, to the Chicago White Sox. To his credit, Mack attempted to exploit the situation faced by the owners by purchasing Cleveland Indians star second baseman Napoleon Lajoie. Lajoie, like Collins, was one of the greatest players ever to play second base. Unfortunately, the forty year-old Lajoie was not only thirteen years older than Collins but was also in the very last days of his stellar career. Lajoie would prove to be a poor substitute for Collins, who was in the prime of his career and who would lead his new team to two League Championships before the decade was over. As the 1915 season progressed, Mack virtually gave away two of the young crown jewels of his pitching staff, Shawkey and Pennock. At midyear it was Barry's turn to be sold, this time to the Boston Red Sox. Before the next season would begin, Frank Baker would also be given up in yet another cash transaction. By opening day of the 1916 season, the only remaining member of the once vaunted $100,000 infield was Stuffy McInnis, who himself would part company with the team just two seasons later.

Rise and Fall

The results of Mack's housecleaning were stark and immediate. The Athletics went from back-to-back League Championships to being dead last in the American League, losing 109 games in the process. Just when it appeared that they had hit bottom, they proceeded to lose 117 games in 1916, a record of futility that required a change to a 162 game schedule and almost ninety years to break.

The fall of the great Philadelphia Athletic dynasty of 1910-1914 was a dramatic one. Their plunge from best to worst in their league was a unique reaction to the harsh economic reality of their times. This story becomes even more profound when considering that the very same script would be played out again for the very same franchise six decades later, as once again a fundamental change in the economics of professional baseball would turn a dominant, dynastic franchise into a basement dweller. For Mack and his Athletics of 1915 the change was temporary. The Federal League, unable to thrive in the new economic climate that they themselves had caused, folded after the 1915 season. In the ensuing anti-trust litigation that would follow, Major League Baseball had come out even stronger than before, solidifying the grip that owners had on their players. The elimination of the competition from the Federal League and the economic impact of the entry of the United States into World War I resulted in player salaries dropping dramatically. Major League Baseball returned to the status quo that had existed before the Federal League threat, and owners like Mack were free to rebuild without the pressure of a challenge to their way of life. When the Athletic dynasty of the 1970s would end, Major League Baseball owners would not be so fortunate. Unlike the decline and fall of Mack's

The $100,000 Infield - Prelude to Déjà Vu

Athletics of 1910-1914, the end of that later dynasty marked the true end of an era. When the championship Athletic teams of the 1970s unraveled, the historical fabric of baseball unraveled with it, ushering in an entirely new and different game.

Fate

On the afternoon of Thursday, March 10, 1960, industrialist Arnold M. Johnson was driving his car through the streets of West Palm Beach, Florida. Johnson had spent the morning reviewing the progress of one of his prime investments – the Kansas City Athletics baseball team, for whom he had been the majority owner since purchasing the team from the Mack family in 1954. Only 53 years old on that March afternoon, Johnson was suddenly stricken with a cerebral hemorrhage. He died in a local hospital later that day, leaving behind a wife, two young children, and a bottom-dwelling baseball team that would now be in search of a new owner.

The Arbiter

On December 23, 1975, independent arbiter Peter Seitz published a decision that would change the balance of owner / player power forever. Seitz was selected to chair a three-member panel to review labor grievances lodged by two Major League Baseball players – Dodger star Andy Messersmith and the recently retired Dave McNally. On the panel with Seitz were representatives of the Major League Baseball owners and the Major League Baseball Players Association, the union established by the players in the 1960s to represent their collective interests in dealing with ownership. It was correctly assumed that in this case, as with any case involving these two constantly warring sides, each representative would interpret the facts in favor of the specific stakeholder that they represented. It therefore fell to Seitz, as the designated "independent" member and chairman of the review panel, to make the final decision.

Though the cases of Messersmith and McNally each had their unique attributes, each was centered on Section 10 A of the standard players contract, the negotiated Agreement between the Players Association and the club owners upon which every individual player contract was based. Section 10 A was referred to as the "renewal clause" of the Basic Agreement. The renewal clause stated:

"If prior to March 1, the Player and the Club have not agreed upon the terms of the contract, then on or before 10 days after said March 1, the Club shall have the right by written notice to the Player to renew this contract for the period of one year."

Rise and Fall

The key phrase in this statement is "for the period of one year." One year. Judging by the history of owner / player relations and the phrase "the *Club* shall have the *right*", it is reasonable to assume that the owners felt that this section served their interests as another tool to pressure players to reach a negotiated agreement on their contract lest the owner force the terms through the renewal clause at their sole discretion. Little did the owners know that this approach would backfire against them and eventually open a Pandora's box that would change the sport forever.

Messersmith and McNally were among a group of approximately nine players to have their contracts automatically renewed by their clubs prior to the start of the 1975 season. As the season progressed, all of the parties except Messersmith and McNally had reached agreement with their teams on new contracts. McNally retired from baseball in June, frustrated by the sudden decline in his once great pitching abilities; for him, a new contract would have been moot. Messersmith finished the season with the Los Angeles Dodgers without signing a new contract. Grievances were filed on behalf of both players at the conclusion of the season and the Seitz panel was asked to make a determination based upon two conflicting positions – the owners position that the term "one year" meant that contracts would be renewed for a single season, but that the player was still bound by the club's "reserve" and that the process could be repeated an infinite number of times, and the players position that one year meant literally that it was a one time event and that a player was no longer considered bound to that club at the end of that year if a new contract was not negotiated and agreed to.

The Arbiter

Both the players and the owners recognized the high stakes involved in the outcome of these cases. Ewing Kaufman, the owner of the Kansas City Royals, petitioned the Federal Judiciary for an injunction against the grievance process, noting that the bulk of his investment was tied up in his most important asset, his players, and that he made that investment with the strict understanding that baseball's reserve system protected his investment by binding players to his club for life. Kaufman, like the other owners, recognized that a ruling in favor of the players would effectively end the reserve system and drive salaries up by a dramatic amount. The Players Association likewise petitioned to the courts to allow the grievance process to proceed and a Federal Court directed that the process continue. After lengthy hearings, Seitz issued a decision in favor of the players, interpreting the language of the Basic Agreement to mean that a player was free to sign with any team after he went through the one-year contract renewal process. Again the owners appealed to the judiciary, and again they were rebuffed. After suffering for decades under the reserve clause, Major League Baseball players could now confidently envision performing their trade with the benefits of free agency, the right to play for whatever team they chose.

As it turned out, neither the players nor the owners knew immediately how to deal with the new landscape. The owners were of course petrified of the impact on their costs brought about by the upheaval of the salary structure that unrestricted free agency could bring. For their part, the players were also concerned that an unrestrained glut of free agents in the market would bring about short-term increases in salaries, but the laws of supply and demand would eventually suppress potential salary increases, particularly for players below superstar status. Both parties therefore recognized that if the reserve clause was dead and free agency was going to be a reality that it needed to be regulated. With this basic understanding in place, ownership and the Players Association negotiated a new Basic Agreement prior to the 1976 season. Under the terms of the new Agreement, the rules pertaining to the new free agent system were developed. These rules specified a minimum length of service that players had to provide to the team that signed them as amateurs before they would be eligible for free agency. This addressed the owners' legitimate concern that they invest significant funds in developing player talent and that they needed some minimum level of protection of and return on that investment before a player could walk out the door. Restrictions were also placed on the number of teams a free agent could negotiate with; a condition intended to partially stem the uncontrollable increase in salaries. As a concession, the owners raised the minimum salary and expanded salary arbitration and trade approval rights for a portion of the players not eligible for immediate free agency.

As a result of the 1976 Basic Agreement, a significant number of players could look toward the 1977 season as the first time in their professional lives that they would be free to voluntarily abandon the team that "owned" them and negotiate with new clubs of their choice. In addition, the cost to sign and retain the most talented players in the game would immediately and dramatically increase.

The players that would benefit the most from this new world were the superstars of the day – players in the prime of their careers with a track record of personal success and the intangible benefits of having played on winning teams. Some teams would also benefit – teams that had more discretionary funds to spend on immediately acquiring top talent and that were fueled by an intense desire to win championships that had eluded them under the previous, restrictive system of building teams through player development and trades. Teams like the New York Yankees, the California Angels, and the Atlanta Braves were ready, able, and willing to stop at nothing to acquire top talent, no matter what the cost.

At the opposite end of the spectrum were teams that already had top players; teams that were already champions, teams that did not have the financial resources to compete annually on the open market for star players, and teams that had previously and successfully relied on developing talent from within and supplementing that talent with a relatively few but cleverly constructed trades.

The Oakland Athletics were such a team.

The Rise

The Johnson Years

After the dismantling of the $100,000 Infield, Connie Mack set about rebuilding his ballclub. The result was a rejuvenated team that from 1925-1933 finished no lower than third place in the American League, a period highlighted by a League Championship in 1931 and back-to-back World Championships in 1929-1930. The quality of Mack's teams from this era is further highlighted by the consideration that three times during that period they were preceded in the standings only by New York Yankee teams that are considered to this day to be among the greatest in baseball history, including the legendary 1927 Murderer's Row team. That great, nine season run ended much as the 1910-1914 run had ended – with the dismantling of the core of the team through a virtual fire sale of the most important players in the franchise. This time it was the Great Depression that emptied Mack's coffers and forced him to sell off his star-laden roster. On a single day in December 1933, Mack sold not one but two future Hall of Famers, Mickey Cochrane and Lefty Grove. Hall of Fame sluggers Al Simmons and Jimmie Foxx also joined the exodus as Mack unloaded his superstars in return for second-tier players and an infusion of much-needed cash. The result was similar to the World War I years for the franchise. By 1935 the once-great team had plunged to the very bottom of the American League standings. In the sixteen seasons from 1935-1950, the Philadelphia Athletics finished dead last ten times and next-to-last two others, finishing as high as fourth place only once. After the 1950 season Mack, now eighty-seven years old, gave up his duties as field manager after an unprecedented half century as the skipper of the Athletics, a record for longevity unlikely to be broken.

Rise and Fall

Mack and his family continued to own the franchise, but by 1954 the family had split regarding the future of the team and the franchise was bleeding money with no relief in sight. Connie Mack, the patriarch of the family and of the Athletics' franchise, had turned over primary control of the family business to his sons, but there was divided counsel over what to do with the club. As the team's financial fortunes continued to decline, the Mack's had little choice but to put their interest in the team up for sale. Numerous investors interested in keeping the franchise in Philadelphia worked to structure a financial package acceptable to all of the relevant parties, but in the end it became clear to all that it was not economically viable for the franchise to remain in Philadelphia. Potential buyers from a number of American cities tendered offers for the club, with the expectation that the franchise would move. Among those interested in buying the team was a group from Chicago that included insurance man Charles O. Finley, a man that would eventually figure prominently in the Athletics' story. But in the end it was Arnold M. Johnson who submitted the winning bid. Johnson received approval from the American League not only to purchase the franchise, but also to move it to Kansas City, Missouri for the 1955 season. By the time the financing deals involving the team, the stadium, and the land upon which the stadium sat were complete, Johnson had become the owner of a major league franchise with zero net cash investment.

Arnold Johnson was not a stranger to Major League Baseball. He already had a well-established business relationship with the New

The Johnson Years

York Yankees. Johnson was in fact the Yankees' landlord, as he was the owner of the iconic Yankee Stadium, as well as Blues Stadium in Kansas City, the home of a Yankee farm team. Johnson's relationship with the Yankees was a great cause of concern to the other American League teams. The complex nature of the business dealings between the parties, shrouded in mystery and secrecy, led some to fear a conflict of interest that could arise if two teams in the same league somehow colluded to assist each other. Johnson was required to shed his formal ties with the Yankees, including sale of Yankee Stadium, as a condition of approval for the purchase of the Athletics, but rumors of an unethical collaboration between Johnson and his Yankee counterparts persisted throughout the 1950's.

The Athletics of Kansas City faired little better than their immediate Philadelphia predecessors. After climbing to sixth place in the first season that Johnson owned the team, the Athletics failed to finish higher than seventh in the eight-team American League in the remaining years that Johnson owned the club. Part of this continued period of poor performances had to do with the fact that the Mack family, with their constant financial constraints, had invested little in scouting for amateur talent or in their minor league system. The franchise was thus unable to stock the major league team with enough quality ballplayers to compete against the strong teams in the American League.

Despite their poor track record, it was not the stigma of losing that was the trademark of the Athletics during the Johnson years.

Rise and Fall

Instead, it was the peculiar role that the Athletics played as a source of talent for the rival New York Yankees. The Yankees reigned as the champions of the American League in eight out of ten seasons during the decade of the fifties, a record of success that spilled into the 1960's as the team began that decade with an additional five straight League Championships. From the time Johnson purchased the Athletics, the two teams became frequent trade partners. The great Yankee champions of the late fifties and early sixties featured a large number of prominent players that had been acquired in a plethora of deals with the Athletics, prompting the Athletics to be given the unflattering label of a "Yankees farm team". In truth, some baseball historians have proposed that on the whole it was the Athletics that actually received the greatest benefit from these trades. But since the World Series annually featured a host of former Athletics in Yankee uniforms while the current Athletics sat home after yet another season at the bottom of the standings, it was difficult to convince those who followed the sport during that period that the talent drain went from New York to Kansas City and not the other way around. In a typical example, the great 1961 World Championship Yankee roster featured former Athletics Clete Boyer, Roger Maris, Hector Lopez, Ralph Terry, Bob Cerv, Ryne Duren, and Joe DeMaestri. Worse still were the rumors that Johnson's Athletics were clandestinely assisting the Yankees in avoiding restrictions related to signing and stockpiling minor league talent, restrictions specifically designed to prevent teams like the Yankees from creating an unfair advantage over other teams. This charge of collusion reached a peak when Johnson himself was called to testify before a United States Congressional

The Johnson Years

hearing on the matter in 1957. Despite wide speculation, none of the charges were ever proven.

And so it was that a pattern seemed to develop. The Athletics would sign and develop young talent, only to ship those players off to the Yankees and other competitors around the league. The Athletics themselves wallowed in the second division, and the club was marked by an instability caused by the constant turnover of players and the certainty of losing season after losing season. It was a pattern that would continue right through Johnson's untimely and unexpected demise in West Palm Beach in 1960.

After more than a half century of ownership by the Mack family, the Johnson era would end after less than six years. Once again, the team was put up for sale. This time, the buyer would not be a well-connected baseball insider, but the ultimate outsider, an iconoclast that would change the Athletics' stodgy, tradition-bound franchise, and indeed Major League Baseball, forever.

The New Owner

He was an enigma. He was a star athlete in his youth, but a terrible disease robbed him of his athletic abilities in the midst of his physical prime. He was a mysterious open book. He virtually invented a whole sector in the group insurance industry, but made his name as a financially unsuccessful owner of his era's greatest baseball team. He devised initiatives that contributed to the wealth of his contemporaries, but was universally despised by them. He painstakingly built a winning sports franchise from the ground up, then effectively destroyed it overnight. He lived life on his own unique terms, yet found those in authority around him constantly battling to reset those terms. He drove Hall of Famers Reggie Jackson, Rollie Fingers, and Catfish Hunter from the fold, yet elicited loyalty and coaxed multiple tours with his team from relative unknowns like Dick Green, Dal Maxvill, Larry Haney, Lew Krausse, and John Donaldson.

His name was Charles Oscar Finley, and he was the man who bought the Kansas City Athletics from the heirs of Arnold Johnson.

Charlie Finley was a self-made millionaire, having built an insurance empire from nothing. Armed with his newly made fortune, Finley set out to fulfill his lifelong dream of owning a baseball team. He was among the bidders when the Mack family put the Athletics up for sale in 1954, ultimately losing out to Arnold Johnson. Finley tried again two years later when the Detroit Tigers were on the block; again he lost out. Two more years passed before Finley embarked on his third attempt

The New Owner

to secure a franchise – this time the object of his desire was the Chicago White Sox, Finley's hometown team. Again Finley lost out. Finley next attempted to win the bid for the expansion Los Angles Angels in 1960. Again Finley's efforts were fruitless. Undaunted, Finley tried again. This time Finley's target was the Kansas City Athletics. At long last his efforts were rewarded, as Charlie Finley became the majority owner of the Kansas City franchise prior to the start of the 1961 season for a relatively meager investment of $2 million. By the time Finley sold his ballclub less than two decades later, a single star player would cost more than what he initially paid for the entire team.

From the start, Finley was at odds with his fellow owners. Finley found them lost in the past way of doing things, wedded to quaint traditions that were revered by diehard fans of the game but that did not fit the modern era.

Throughout his days as the Athletics' owner, Finley brought forward a series of initiatives that he felt would add to fan interest in the game, ultimately serving to increase revenues for the owners. Finley's ideas were almost uniformly met with howls of derision from his fellow owners and often from the public. But despite the initial resistance, many were eventually implemented. Changes suggested or supported by Finley included:

Selecting players for the Hall of Fame while they were still active.

Shorter schedules.

Rise and Fall

Inter-league play.

Nighttime World Series games.

Designated hitters.

Designated runners.

Three-ball walks and two-strike strikeouts.

Brightly colored baseballs and bats.

Brightly colored uniforms.

Red, white, and blue bases.

Finley was persistent and passionate in support of his proposals. In a 1963 letter to Major League Baseball Commissioner Ford Frick, Finley advocated for nighttime weekday World Series games. Finley correctly observed, "Football would never play a championship game on a weekday afternoon." Working people were almost completely shut out from following the fall classic due to the tradition of playing all post-season games in daylight. It was a logical argument, but it would take another eight years before the concept would be tried.

While his relationships with his fellow owners and baseball's executive management were rocky at best, Finley's relationships with his employees could best be described as bizarre. Sandwiched as he was between the past, as symbolized by Connie Mack's dual role of

The New Owner

Athletics' owner and manager, and the future, symbolized by the hands-on role of activist owners such as Atlanta's Ted Turner and the Yankees George Steinbrenner, Finley was a strange anomaly among owners in the 1960's. When he purchased the team he espoused humility when it came to his knowledge of the game of baseball, pledging to hire the very best front office talent available and empowering that talent to run his baseball operations. If he was sincere at the time of making those statements, his attitude quickly changed. Never a man to sit idly by while others made important strategic and tactical decisions that impacted his most prized asset, Finley soon exerted tyrannical control over every single detail of the operations of the Athletics' franchise. For a time he even eliminated the role of general manager, reserving for himself the responsibility of that position. Upon purchasing the ballclub, Finley once boasted, "I may be outsmarted, but I'll never be out hustled." This pledge he did keep – friend and foe alike marveled at how he threw himself into the full-time job of running his baseball team. No detail was too small or insignificant to escape his direct attention. Finley demanded a similar display of attentiveness, dedication, and above all else loyalty from every single employee on his payroll, including his field personnel and particularly his managers. The use of the plural "managers" is intentional. Unable to find the required balance of competence, performance, loyalty, and initiative, Finley would change managers on a near constant basis. After hiring Joe Gordon to manage his ballclub prior to the 1961 season, Finley proceeded to fire Gordon just sixty games into the season. It was a maneuver that Finley would perfect in the subsequent two decades. From 1961 to 1980, Finley would change managers seventeen times. Seven of those changes would come during the regular season. After being fired by Finley, three men would find themselves agreeing to serve second terms as Finley's manager, only to be fired for a second time. Finley's relationships with his managers quickly became the stuff of legends. As early as 1961, Joe Gordon allegedly made a sarcastic note on a lineup card stating that it was "approved by COF", indicating that the lineup had been approved by the owner. In his own defense, Finley pointed out that what others characterized as interference with his managerial staff was simply the offering of "suggestions". Failure to abide by these helpful tidbits undoubtedly contributed to many of the seventeen managerial changes that took place in the twenty years that Finley owned the club. Other favorite infractions included perceptions of disloyalty, signs of failure to control the thoughts, attitudes, and behaviors of the players, and any signs of what Finley would consider a "weak backbone". Such infractions would almost immediately cost a manager their job, regardless of their success on the playing field.

Finley's relationship with his players was equally complex. He would personally charm players into signing with his team, and then often treat them with disdain at the first sign of a lack of gratitude. He would extend favorable loans to players to help them address financial difficulties, and then aggressively pursue repayment. He would make loyal players rich by facilitating zero-risk investments personally guaranteed by Finley himself, and then vindictively trade disloyal players to the worst teams in the game with little or no compensation in return. He would reward special performances with cash bonuses, and then negotiate like a miser with those same players at contract time. He

The New Owner

would come across as a father figure to a player one day, and then virtually disown the same player the next. Most of these changes were driven by one of two factors – loyalty and appreciation on the part of the player, and finances. Once he had built a successful championship team, Finley's demeanor toward his players turned more and more negative and eventually served as the basis of his undoing.

Like every human being, Charlie Finley had flaws. It was those flaws that drew the lion's share of attention during his years as the owner of the Athletics. But Finley's accomplishments as the architect of one of history's greatest baseball teams should not be overlooked. Finley wanted a championship for his Athletics, and true to his promise he was never out-hustled or out-maneuvered in his effort to acquire one.

Piece-by-piece, Charlie Finley would personally transform the laughing stock of the American League into one of the most powerful franchises ever.

The Seeds of a Dynasty

The Kansas City Athletics opened their first season under the ownership of Charlie Finley on April 11, 1961. While former Athletics Roger Maris, Clete Boyer, and Hector Lopez prepared to annihilate American League pitching as anchors of the legendary 1961 New York Yankee lineup, the Athletics' starting lineup that day featured former Yankees Jerry Lumpe, Norm Siebern, Marv Throneberry, and Andy Carey. Dick Howser, who would later be recognized as the American League's Rookie of the Year for 1961, was the Athletics' starting shortstop. The catcher was Haywood Sullivan, whose lackluster playing career would later be overshadowed by a successful run as a front-office executive. It was by and large a young lineup, backed by a cadre of other young players and a few grizzled veterans. Four of the nine opening day starters would be gone from the team by mid-season. None of the remaining five would last with the Athletics past 1963. The group included some talented ballplayers; Siebern would go on to be selected for the All Star team four times, Howser twice, and Lumpe once. The team would actively utilize the trading block, but it was generally an exchange for equal or lesser talent and the trade market was hardly the foundation for a winning franchise as even the most resourceful general manager would find it difficult to use this roster of trade material to significantly upgrade the talent level via the traditional trading process.

For Charlie Finley to build a winner, he would have to find another way.

The Seeds of a Dynasty

Far away from Kansas City, the Broncos of Lewiston, Idaho were preparing to begin the Northwest League season in the spring of 1961. The league had a history that dated back as far as that of the American League – all the way to 1901. The affiliation between Lewiston and the Kansas City Athletics had been established the previous season. The Broncos possessed a strong roster for the 1961 season, a roster that included future Kansas City Athletics Jack Aker, John O'Donoghue, Billy Bryan, and Ossie Chavarria. Lewiston manager John McNamara served double-duty as one of the team's catchers. McNamara would never make the major leagues as a player, but he would go on to enjoy a long career as a major league manager, a career that included a stint as the manager of the Athletics and a Manager of the Year award in 1986. Like many minor leagues, the Northwest League split their seasons into two halves, with the winner of each half squaring off in a playoff to decide the League Champion. In 1961, Lewiston would go on to win the first half title and fall just one game short of also taking the title for the second half. A victory over the rival Yakima Bears in the post-season playoffs would later give Lewiston the championship.

Anchoring the third base position for Lewiston that season was a bright prospect named Dick Green. The twenty year-old Green had been one of the last players signed by the Johnson regime prior to the 1960 season. After a year in the Florida State League, the young infielder was progressing nicely through the organization. Green had spent the

Rise and Fall

previous season at shortstop, but was finding himself spending most of his time with the Broncos as a third baseman. Displaying great hands and versatility in the field, Green demonstrated that he was also a threat at the plate as he slammed a career high of eighteen home runs to go along with a healthy .273 batting average. Green's performance attracted the attention of Finley and his assistants – for Dick Green, all signs pointed to Kansas City.

While Dick Green continued his professional development in the Northwest League and the Athletics began their inaugural season under their new management, young boys all across America prepared in their own way for another season of their national pastime. In pickup games, Little League, American Legion, PONY, and high school competition, young men everywhere were feeding their special passion for the game of baseball. From the farms of North Carolina to the sandlots of Ohio, the future members of Charlie Finley's first championship team were among those oiling their gloves for the upcoming season. The youngsters in this group included seventeen year-old Sal Bando, fifteen year-olds Dave Duncan, Johnny Odom, Jimmy Hunter, and Rick Monday, fourteen year-olds Gene Tenace, Reggie Jackson, Rollie Fingers, and Joe Rudi, and eleven year-old Vida Blue. For most of this group, rites of male passage such as shaving and a driver's license were still in the future. While Dick Green was climbing up the Athletics' organizational depth chart, these young men were dreaming of a varsity letter. They were quite literally children. Whatever their dreams, none

The Seeds of a Dynasty

of them could have predicted that a decade later they would come together to form the nucleus of a championship team. The seeds of dynasty were not growing in Kansas City's Municipal Stadium, but on baseball diamonds across the United States. Like needles in a nation filled with haystacks, finding these gems and assembling that championship team would take five things – boundless energy, persistence, talent-spotting skills, salesmanship, and money, lots and lots of money.

And no man in the game of baseball was better equipped or better suited for the task than Charles O. Finley.

The Basement

The Finley era picked up right where the Johnson era ended with the Athletics embedded deep in the American League cellar. The team that Finley purchased finished dead last in the standings in 1960, thirty-nine games out of first place and seven games behind their next closest adversary. The good news for 1961 was that the American League was expanding for the first time in its sixty-year history to ten teams. Although there was no concrete evidence available, the theory was that expansion teams would be among the worst teams in the league while they built their talent pool. The Athletics were hopeful that addition of the two new teams would result in at least a slight rise in the standing for the Athletics. It didn't. Once again the team finished in last place, tied with the expansion Washington Senators, an incredible forty-seven and a half games out of first place. It would take the Athletics exactly ten years to make up those forty-seven and a half games and reach the top of the standings.

The issue with the Athletics was fundamental – their players just weren't that good. The 1961 Athletics were last in the league in home runs and earned run average and near the bottom in most other major offensive and pitching categories. In addition to being weak, the Athletics' lineup was also unstable. In order to compensate for his relative lack of baseball management experience, owner Charlie Finley hired Frank Lane, a seasoned baseball executive, to be his general manager. Known by the moniker "Trader Lane", Lane had a well-deserved reputation for engaging in virtually constant trade negotiations. While Lane was truly a master in the art of making trades from a volume

The Basement

perspective, his trades often resulted in little or no net benefit to his team and often hurt his club. In addition, the whirlwind of players coming and going made it impossible for a team to settle into any level of normalcy. While normalcy was not a particularly abundant condition during the Finley years, Lane's maniacal trading habits became too much for even Finley to bear; Trader Lane was fired before his first full season was complete.

On June 8, 1961 Finley laid the very first brick in the foundation that would eventually result in a championship dynasty. It was a small, even tiny step, but one that would set the tone for many more to follow. On that day, Finley paid a record $125,000 to sign high school pitcher Lew Krausse Jr. Krausse was the son of a former Athletics pitcher who now worked as a scout for Finley's organization. The younger Krausse had a sensational high school pitching record, and Finley directed that Krausse forgo minor league seasoning and be placed immediately in the Athletics' starting pitching rotation. This was a tactic that Finley would employ liberally for the next six years; acquire a youngster and educate them at the "School of Hard Knocks" – the major league level. A week later the eighteen year-old made his mound debut, shutting out the expansion Los Angeles Angels on just three hits. His second start came a week later against the Boston Red Sox. Although he lost the game, he did open with six more scoreless innings before tiring in the seventh. It was all down hill from there. In his next five starts the youngster never made it through the sixth inning. He ended the season on a high note with a complete game victory, but it was clear that Krausse was not ready for the major leagues. Krausse would spend all or part of the next

Rise and Fall

four seasons in the minor leagues before joining the Athletics for good in 1965.

The Athletics made slow but somewhat steady improvement over the next two seasons, rising as high as eighth place in the ten-team American League. Each season saw them growing a tiny bit stronger and winning a few more games than the year before. But Finley was growing impatient. Unwilling to wait for the development of his young ballplayers and insanely jealous of the perennial League Champion New York Yankees, Finley incorrectly decided that a few bold steps would accelerate his dream of owning a championship team.

Finley routinely cited the reasons that he felt the Yankees enjoyed an unfair advantage over their opposition. In the winter following the 1963 season, the focus of Finley's Yankee obsession was on their ballpark. The original Yankee Stadium featured one of the shortest right field fences in baseball, an attractive target for left-handed hitters. This feature was offset by a left-center field power alley that was among the farthest distances from home plate in the game. Known as "death valley", this region was the bane of many a right-handed power hitter's existence. Finley claimed that the Yankees were able to use these features to an unfair advantage, allowing them to exploit these features by stocking up on left-handed power hitters and left-handed pitchers. What Finley failed to account for was that the Yankee roster featured many of the very best players in the game. This fact did not dissuade Finley; he would try to beat the Yankees at their own game. The theme of the Kansas City Athletics' 1964 season would be power.

The Basement

Finley ordered that the right field fence be moved in to the same distance as Yankee Stadium's right field line, a move later overruled by the American League office. It was the first of many intercessions by American League management as well as the Major League Baseball Commissioner's office against Finley. Finley moved the fences in to the closest point allowed by league rules and carried out his next step in his quest to quench his "thirst for power". In 1963, the Athletics were ninth in the American League in home runs. To address the power vacuum, Finley traded for veteran sluggers Rocky Colavito and Jim Gentile. Although both were past their prime, their combined home run total of 46 in 1963 was almost half of the total power output of the Athletics. The infusion of home run power did have an effect on the Athletics' offense. The Athletics hit 166 home runs in 1964, four more than the hated Yankees and an increase of 75% over their 1963 output. Unfortunately, short fences benefit opposing teams as much as they do the home club, a situation made even worse when the home club has a pitching staff prone to throwing home run balls. While the Athletics' batters were hitting their 166 home runs, the Athletics' pitchers were giving up 220, the most in the league. The Athletics were outscored 836-621, and the team slid backward to the bottom of the standings, finishing forty-two games behind the same Yankee team that they had out-homered. It was clear that there would be no "quick fix" to building a championship team. 1964 became a painful but important lesson for the impatient owner. The road to a championship would be a long and hard one and would require a completely different approach to building a team, an approach that meant building the roster from the ground up rather than from the outside. With few options for the importation of talent available during the era of the 1960's, a talent problem that had taken decades to create could not be corrected overnight.

Recruiting

Frank Lane believed that you could trade you way to success. Charlie Finley knew better. While his 1961 roster included some excellent ballplayers such as former Yankees Norm Siebern and Jerry Lumpe and 1961 Rookie of the Year Dick Howser, there was not enough of a talent pool to package together to generate a significant advantage through trading. Good baseball trades are the product of dealing from strength and depth to acquire the necessary components to fill in holes and weaknesses; the Athletics did not have the strength or depth to trade from and there were far too many holes and weaknesses to address. Building a contender would be a long, drawn out process that would require a focus on bringing new talent into the organization at the amateur level. With little in the way of a foundation available upon which to build, Finley would have to establish that foundation and build upon it piece-by-piece, player-by-player. Charlie Finley resolved to be the very best recruiter in baseball. Nobody would outwork the Athletics when it came to canvassing the playing fields of America to identify and sign the best amateur players. Finley would spare no expense in acquiring the very best amateur talent available. In addition to his financial arsenal, Finley would also rely on two powerful strengths that he possessed – his ability as a salesman and his energy.

Amateur baseball players that were in a position to select among multiple teams bidding for their services generally selected their team based on some combination of three factors – the size and structure of the financial package the teams offered, the prospects of rapidly establishing themselves in the position of their choice with the major league club, and the location and profile of the team itself. Money spoke the loudest, and many recruits simply signed with the highest bidder. In this regard Finley was particularly well positioned to compete; when Charlie Finley set his sights on a player, he made sure that he was not outbid. The promise of rapid advancement was another effective weapon in Finley's arsenal. With weaknesses on the Athletics' roster plentiful, young players could easily see a clear path to playing at the major league level with minimal or no minor league seasoning. Players who turned Finley down generally did so out of deference to the final consideration – the team location and profile. Clubs like the New York Yankees and Los Angels Dodgers often lured young players into signing with their franchises with the offer of playing for the most successful franchises in the game or playing in marquee cities. Yankee management often touted their long history of post-season success and the prospects of marketing and other off-field fringe benefits as strong selling points for their teams. For many young players, the excitement of playing in a major metropolitan area also outweighed the benefits of playing in the relatively rural Kansas City area. Despite this last point, Charlie Finley generally got the players he wanted.

The first post-season game in the Charlie Finley era of the Athletics' franchise would be played on October 3, 1971. The starting lineup that day included four players (Dick Green, Bert Campaneris, Dave Duncan, and Joe Rudi) that were signed as amateurs either by Finley or immediately before Finley's arrival. Three others (Vida Blue,

Recruiting

Sal Bando, and Reggie Jackson) were the product of the earliest amateur player drafts. Of the remaining two, one (Angel Mangual) was acquired in a trade as a minor leaguer and had split time in 1971 with another amateur draftee (Rick Monday). The last player, Tommy Davis, was a journeyman; apart from Mangual's four at bats with the Pittsburgh Pirates, Davis was the only player in the lineup with previous experience with another major league team.

In his early days as Athletics' owner, Finley set about signing the players that would form the heart of the club's major league roster in the mid-1960's. Lesser-known players such as Aurelio Monteagudo, Bill Landis, Freddie Norman, Rene and Marcel Lachemann, Tony LaRussa, Roberto Rodriguez, Ramon Webster, Tommie Reynolds, Tony Pierce, John Donaldson, and Syd O'Brien were signed by Finley during this era, as were future Athletic stars Bert Campaneris, Joe Rudi, Catfish Hunter, Blue Moon Odom, Jim Nash, and Paul Linblad.

Relying on the input from an excellent corps of scouts, Finley often personally handled the negotiations with his prized high school and college recruiting targets. Finley took great pride in his ability as a deal closer. His reputation and ego suffered blows when highly prized amateur players Willie Crawford and Rick Reichardt opted to take less money than Finley offered to play in California – Crawford with the Dodgers and Reichardt with the Angels. Finley had reportedly offered Crawford $200,000 and Reichardt more than the record $205,000 that he eventually signed for. But such setbacks were the exception rather than the rule. Finley pledged to spend close to a million of his own dollars to secure the best players that money could buy; although the loss of Crawford and Reichardt prevented him from reaching that audacious goal, Charlie Finley outspent every other major league team in the pursuit of amateur players in the mid 1960's.

When it came to bonuses, Finley paid top dollar for his targeted prospects. Like many owners of that era, Finley's generosity was not limited to the bonuses he offered the young athletes he courted. Ever the master salesman, Finley was quick to ascertain what additional tangibles he could use to sweeten the pot for a potential player. Additional incentives ranged from a tuxedo and a rented car for Willie Crawford's senior prom to money for surgery at the Mayo Clinic to repair Catfish Hunter's foot, which was severely damaged in a hunting accident. If Finley liked a young prospect there was virtually no limit to his creativity when it came to enticing a player to sign with his Athletics.

In addition to his commitment to providing the financial incentives necessary to sign key prospects, Finley was also able to make good on the promise of a fast track to the major leagues for several of his young players. This was not always a complete matter of choice for Finley. For years, the lords of baseball harbored grave concerns about the skyrocketing bonuses being paid to sign amateur players. A variety of tactics were devised to suppress bonuses. Major League Baseball made an overt attempt to dissuade clubs from paying high bonuses by forcing clubs to retain a certain number of designated "bonus players" on their major league roster or risk losing the player and the bonus money they paid in a minor league draft. It was recognized that this was not a

Recruiting

viable solution; young players were having their careers damaged by preventing them from getting the minor league experience that they needed to develop, and clubs were routinely engaging in fraudulent activity to disguise the size of the bonuses that they were paying. Under revised rules enacted in 1958, players were still subject to being drafted if they were not on the club's forty-man roster after one year, regardless of the size of their bonus. Clubs therefore still had great incentive to move their most prized prospects up to the major leagues as quickly as possible to avoid the potential of having those players taken in the minor league draft and thus losing out on their investment. In addition, Finley's Athletics featured a roster full of holes; even the youngest, most inexperienced players could not be much worse than the "seasoned" players currently playing for the team. Finley did try to hide some of his best prospects. Although Catfish Hunter spent the entire 1964 season on the disabled list due to his foot surgery, the fact that he was under contract for the season made him eligible for the minor league draft in 1965 if he was not kept on the Athletics' major league roster. Charlie Finley tried to convince Hunter to sign a new contract that was dated a year after the original (Hunter wisely refused). Hunter progressed straight to the Athletics in 1965 having never played an inning of minor league baseball. Finley also ordered Jim Nash's first minor league manager to literally hide Nash during his first professional season at Daytona Beach; the young pitcher was forbidden to appear in uniform on the field in 1963, and his baseball activities were limited to occasionally warming up in a bullpen if and only if there were no opposing scouts in the area. By doing so, Nash was available to play the full 1964 season at

Rise and Fall

the minor league level, with his anonymity offsetting the risk of his potential selection in the minor league draft.

Such silliness aside, many players did move quickly to the Athletics' roster under more traditional circumstances. Nash's Daytona Beach teammate Dave Duncan spent all of 1964 with Kansas City, although he appeared in only twenty-five games. Such limited action was often the case for young prospects protected on the major league roster under these circumstances. A year later it was valued catching prospect Rene Lachemann's turn to rise to the major league roster after a single season in the minors. Don Buschhorn was considered one of the organization's top pitching prospects, but a few games on the Athletics' mound in 1965 so rattled the youngster that he never overcame the ensuing stage fright and vanished from the major league scene forever. One of Finley's biggest bonus recipients, infielder Skip Lockwood, also joined the club in 1965 after a half season in the minor leagues. Lockwood was a disaster at the plate, a situation he later claimed was caused by bad eyesight. With the arrival of super prospect Sal Bando to the Athletics in 1965, Lockwood's days as the "third baseman of the future" were clearly numbered. When Lockwood returned to the major leagues with another organization four years later it was as a pitcher. Joe Rudi was an example of what happened when key prospects weren't fast-tracked to the big club; Rudi was taken from the Athletics by the Cleveland Indians in the minor league draft in the spring of 1965, forcing Finley to reacquire him via a trade at the end of that same season. Minor league prospect Felix Millan was also lost to the Athletics in a similar manner; Millan would surface years later as a star second baseman for

Recruiting

the Atlanta Braves and the New York Mets and a 1973 World Series opponent of the Athletics.

While the highly paid bonus rookies made their early, fleeting appearances with the Athletics, two young players arrived almost unnoticed in 1964. Having completed his steady climb through the organization, Dick Green joined the Athletics as a September call-up in 1963 and took over as the club's starting second baseman in 1964. It was a role that he would hold for most of the next eleven seasons. Green was a versatile, sure handed infielder with a solid bat who served as a rock of stability during a very unstable period in the club's history. Green's play caught the attention of the American League opposition and was seen as a sign that Finley's ballclub was on the rise. The second new arrival was utility player Bert Campaneris, who joined the team in July. Campaneris split his time between shortstop, third base, and left field, showing signs of the sensational player that he was to become. Signed for a miniscule bonus in comparison to many of his teammates, Campaneris would provide Finley with a massive return on his investment in the years to come.

With the promotion of Green and Campaneris to the big club, Charlie Finley had perhaps unknowingly laid a critical part of the foundation for his team's future success. Homegrown talent would provide the fuel for one of the greatest teams in the history of baseball. The first parts of a future champion were in place.

Rule IV

Until the Seitz decision in 1975, professional baseball players were bound for life to the team that originally signed them. This was referred to as holding a player's "reserve". Player had little control over their destiny during this period. If a player no longer wanted to play for the franchise that owned them, they could always retire. Another option was to demand a trade, their only leverage being the retirement threat. This scenario often played out during contract negotiations during the off season. When faced with a contract offer deemed by the player to be unacceptably low, the player could simply refuse to sign a contract and "hold out". Of course, they were restricted from playing for or even talking to any other professional baseball team. Often such an impasse would last into the spring or in some cases even into the regular season, at which time either the player or the team would ultimately give in. The restriction binding a player to his team existed even after a player's retirement, and could be severed only with the granting of a release by the owning ballclub.

Another way for a player to escape from a franchise was to be traded to or drafted by another team. Trading and selling players has been a common fixture of the sport ever since there has been professional baseball. The drafting of professional players has also been a long-standing aspect of the game, albeit one that gets far less publicity than the higher profile player trades due to the fact that (with the exception of expansion drafts) the drafting of players is limited to players not on the major league roster. The minor league draft, known as the Rule V Draft, was instituted as a safeguard to prevent top teams from stockpiling talent

Rule IV

in their minor league systems, removing that talent from the pool available to other teams. The concern was that teams would sign players, thus achieving permanent ownership of their reserve, then bury them in their farm system, recalling them to the major league club only in an emergency. Although the terms of the Rule V draft changed slightly over the years, they basically provided an option for major league teams to draft players from the minor league rosters of their competitors with the understanding that they would keep that player on their own major league roster. One of the more famous cases of the Rule V Draft occurred in 1954, when the Pittsburgh Pirates drafted young Roberto Clemente from the Brooklyn Dodgers.

All of the restrictions cited above applied to *professional* baseball players whose reserve was already owned by a professional baseball team. Amateur players, individuals in high school, college, or others that had not yet been signed by a major league club, were not owned by anybody and were thus free to sign with whatever team they wished. Ironically, these amateurs were baseball's first free agents. And as a foretaste of things to come, major league owners bid generously for the services of the cream of the amateur free agent crop, driving up the cost to acquire the services of these young players.

While owners were steadily driving up the cost of amateur free agents, they simultaneously recognized that the escalating bonuses being paid to unproven talent was impacting their collective bottom line. In response to the escalation of amateur bonuses, the owners began erecting a number of safeguards to try to stem the bonus growth. The strongest deterrent involved Rule V draft eligibility, which was intended to dissuade clubs from paying excessive bonuses for players that were unlikely to rapidly progress to the major league roster. When the specter of Rule V failed to bring bonuses into control, new limitations were added forbidding the demotion of players who had received large bonuses in the hope that teams would not want to clog their major league roster with talent that was unprepared for the big leagues. These restrictions failed miserably. Unscrupulous club owners routinely cheated by misrepresenting bonus amounts or by hiding bonus payments. Clubs would also accept the risk of simply signing players with the bonuses necessary to secure their services, then putting them on the major league roster where they would often bide their time in the obscurity of a major league bench until they had seasoned to the point at which they could play regularly at the major league level. As a result, young players with high potential were rushed to the major leagues at the expense of the critical minor league experience necessary to hone their raw skills. In addition, the teams were burdened with tying up roster spots for players that were of no immediate value. And all the while the bonuses paid to these young men continued to increase at an alarming rate. Without any realistic controls in place, owners with the capability to invest in amateur players would spare no expense to get the players that they wanted, driving up the cost of amateur free agents for all of the teams. Soon, top prospects were taking home bonuses that were the equivalent of many years of salary for established major league players. The owners, armed with the one-sided bargaining position enabled by the reserve clause, were depressing major league salaries while the signing

Rule IV

bonuses for amateur players were spiraling out of control. And nobody played this paradoxical game better than Charles O. Finley.

While establishing a reputation for a fanatical obsession with his bottom line, Finley's interest in spending top dollar when it came to investing in amateur talent was a result of his recognition that there was no better alternative available to build a winning major league team. Finley did not have the players at the major league level to crack the upper echelon of the league, nor did he have the talent within the organization to package together for trades to acquire the necessary talent. Since his success depended upon developing a roster of top-notch players, and since the materials for developing that roster did not exist within the organization when Finley bought the team, the only option available was to begin at the beginning and invest at the amateur level. Finley personally supervised the scouting and the negotiations with many of the amateur players signed by the Athletics. If Finley coveted a player, the Athletics typically either signed him or were at least on the short list of finalists that the player considered. Of the twenty-five players on the 1971 roster of the divisional champion Athletics, eleven were amateur free agents signed by the Finley regime from 1961-1965.

Signs that the bonus situation was out of control dated back as early as 1950. That year the Pittsburgh Pirates paid high school pitcher Paul Pettit a bonus of $100,000 in a convoluted deal that included a movie contract. At the time, the Pirate's Ralph Kiner was the proud owner of the highest salary in the National League. Kiner's salary of $65,000 a year was $35,000 less than the bonus paid to Pettit. The

Rise and Fall

$100,000 ceiling was matched, but not exceeded, for another seven years until Bob "Hawk" Taylor, future journeyman catcher, was paid $112,000 by the Braves. The ante continued to rise, culminating in a $175,000 payout by the pioneering Pirates to Bob Bailey in 1961. The Bailey case signaled a wakeup call to the owners and was a clear sign that there was no end in sight for the spiraling bonuses being paid by desperate teams. The final straw came in 1964 when the Los Angeles Angels broke the $200,000 bonus plateau, signing Rick Reichardt for a reported $205,000. It was also reported that Finley had outbid the Angels, but that Reichardt took less money to play in the Los Angeles area. Finley also reportedly bid $200,000 for Willie Crawford, who later signed for a significantly lesser sum to play for the Los Angeles Dodgers. Although he never broke a bonus record, Finley did pay Lew Krausse a $125,000 signing bonus in 1961 and Skip Lockwood a $100,000 bonus in 1964. Many other players benefited from Finley's desire to secure the very best amateur free agents as the seed corn to cultivate his dream of a championship team. Some, like Lockwood, flopped and provided virtually no return on Finley's investment. Others, like Catfish Hunter, returned the value of his $75,000 bonus many times over.

While bonus payments continued to grow, baseball's owner community struggled with an almost annual tweaking of the bonus / draft system. Some owners, convinced that the peripheral and cosmetic changes to the process would never address the core issue of escalating bonuses, lobbied annually for an amateur free agent draft. In the winter of 1965 they got their wish. The amateur free agent era ended on June 8, 1965 when the first Rule IV Draft was held. Once drafted, an amateur

Rule IV

player had the option of signing with the club that drafted him or sitting out until the following draft. High school seniors, armed with the option of enrolling in a college program and further developing their skills, had the greatest leverage, college seniors the least. Under the original Rule IV process, players that did not sign were eligible for a "supplemental" draft the following January. The primary concept behind the draft was to limit the options for the amateur free agents, thus suppressing their negotiating position and restricting the growth of signing bonuses. Another goal of the process was to alter the balance of power away from dominant franchises such as the Yankees and Dodgers in favor of the weaker teams. This would be accomplished by giving the worst teams from the previously completed season the first picks in each round of the draft. The two leagues would trade off the right to own the very first pick in the draft, with the American League drafting first in odd-numbered years and the National League picking first in the even-numbered years.

Based upon their last-place finish in 1964, the honor of making the first pick in the first amateur free agent draft in June 1965 went to the Kansas City Athletics.

The Athletics used their historic first pick to select outfielder Rick Monday, a record-setting member of the NCAA champion Arizona State University baseball program. Monday had turned down a $20,000 bonus from both the Dodgers and the Yankees after of high school. As an enticement to Monday, Finley negotiated a signing bonus of $100,000 after he was drafted. Finley had the player he wanted, and baseball observers generally agreed that the draft concept had met its primary goal – Monday's bonus, as significant as it was, was probably half of what he would have received in an open market. Finley pointed to the bonus with pride, insisting that it proved that he was a fair man that would pay a player what he perceived as their full worth.

Other first-round picks of that historic first draft included future twenty game winner Joe Coleman (the third overall pick), future Athletics Billy Conigliaro and Ray Fosse (the fifth and seventh picks, respectively), and 1970 National League Rookie of the Year Bernie Carbo (the sixteenth overall pick). In the second round, the Athletics passed over a young catcher named Johnny Bench (eventually the thirty-sixth overall pick by the Cincinnati Reds) to select Joe Keough, the younger brother of major leaguer Marty Keough, himself a bonus baby some years earlier. It is hard to imagine the impact that Bench might have had on the Athletics' lineup, particularly during their second-place finishes in 1969, 1970, and 1976 when Bench was in his prime. Despite the Bench oversight, the Athletics had a successful first draft, drafting future stars Sal Bando (Rick Monday's Arizona State teammate and the 1965 College World Series Most Valuable Player, a sixth round draft pick) and Gene Tenace (a twentieth round pick), in addition to Monday. Other future stars selected in that first draft included Andy Messersmith, Ken Holtzman, Tom Seaver, Nolan Ryan, and Carlton Fisk. Some, like Seaver and Fisk, declined to sign and were later re-drafted by the teams for whom they would make their mark. Others, like Monday, Holtzman, and Ryan, would begin their major league careers as early as 1966. No fewer than eight of the players selected in the draft came from the roster

Rule IV

of Arizona State University, including Monday, Bando, and future major leaguer Duffy Dyer. The Athletics were one of only six teams to stay in the draft until the forty-eighth round. The Athletics also participated in the short-lived supplemental draft of American Legion players that August, a draft which delivered future Athletic Earl Williams to the Milwaukee Braves.

In the second Rule IV draft in June 1966, the Athletics once again received the first American League pick as a "reward" for another last place finish the previous season. In 1966 it was the National League's turn to pick first. Like Finley and the Athletics, the last place New York Mets had focused on a handful of marquee players as they planned their draft strategy. One of the top players eligible for the 1966 draft was a slugging outfielder from Arizona State University named Reggie Jackson. Another was a California high school catcher named Steve Chilcott. Chilcott was personally scouted by Casey Stengel, who had become a Vice President in the Mets front office upon his retirement as manager of the team in 1965. Chilcott received rave reviews from Stengel, whose opinion carried a lot of weight within the organization. The Mets were in need of a first class catcher as an answer to the revolving door that had existed at that position since their inception. At the time they had little cause to foresee that the current occupant of the catcher spot in the Met lineup, Jerry Grote, would be a fixture at the position for the next several years, or that Chilcott would be an absolute flop. In a move that has been labeled as one of the historic blunders in the history of sports drafts, the Mets selected Chilcott. The delighted Finley then made Reggie Jackson the second player to be selected in the draft. Other than Jackson and fifth round selection Dave Hamilton, the 1966 draft had little impact on the Athletics' future roster. But the selection of Jackson made it all worthwhile. As of 2008, Steve Chilcott is the only non-pitcher ever selected as the first pick in the draft not to play in a regular season, major league game (the unfortunate Brien Taylor, a pitcher selected by the New York Yankees in 1991, is the only other number one pick never to make it to the majors). Had the Mets selected Reggie Jackson rather than Chilcott, it is possible that this book may have been about a New York Met dynasty and the future Athletics' championship teams would likely have never come to pass.

Throughout his early years as owner of the Athletics, Finley employed all of the tools at his disposal to acquire players to the very best of his ability. Finley was a primary character in the story of the birth of the amateur free agent draft. He benefited by the system put in place in reaction to the excesses of the owners through the fruits of his team's position at the bottom of the standings and through his effective scouting of the nation's top talent. Finley had survived a fundamental change in the relationship between one class of players and the owners that controlled them. One aspect of player free agency was closed forever. The next three times that the topic of free agency would make the headlines, Finley would again be intimately involved. In each of those cases, the outcome would not be one that would please the Athletics' owner.

Building and Rebuilding

With the debacle of the 1964 power push behind them, the Athletics set about the process of once again reinventing themselves and rebuilding their roster. The transition would be gradual and, in stark contrast to the early sixties, the newcomers would come largely from within the organization's farm system, stocked as it was by Charlie Finley's steady signing of young bonus players.

As a sign of the departure from the focus on big name power hitters that defined the 1964 season, the only major transaction the club completed in the off season was to unload Rocky Colavito to the Cleveland Indians in a complicated three-way trade that also included the Chicago White Sox. In return, the Athletics received some much needed pitching help in the presence of Fred Talbot as well as outfielders Jim Landis and Mike Hershberger, both of whom were widely rated among the very finest defensive outfielders in the game. Their presence along side of youngsters Jose Tartabull and Tommie Reynolds gave the Athletics one of the strongest defensive outfields in the league.

The lineup change that had the greatest long-term impact on the fortunes of the franchise was the establishment of Bert Campaneris as an every day player. Campaneris spent the early weeks of the 1965 season as the Athletics' left fielder, eventually returning to his natural position of shortstop in early June, a role that he would fill for the next eleven seasons. Campaneris possessed a weapon that was virtually absent from the A's arsenal in 1964 – speed. The entire Athletics team stole a total of 34 bases in 1964; with Campaneris in the daily lineup that number more than tripled for 1965, with Campaneris leading the team and the

Rise and Fall

American League with 51 steals. Campaneris would go on to lead the league in steals six times in the eight seasons from 1965-1972. As the primary table-setter for the Athletics' lineup, Campaneris would serve as one of the most potent forces in the Athletics' offensive arsenal. At bat and especially on the bases, Bert Campaneris made things happen.

Campaneris was also at the center of one of owner Charlie Finley's more unusual promotional events in 1965. Playing off of the excitement that the speedy shortstop brought to the ballclub, Finley decided to promote Campaneris' versatility by proclaiming the September 8 game against the California Angels "Bert Campaneris Night". To highlight the evening, Campaneris would be the first player in major league history to play all nine positions in a single game. With the team in last place, thirty-five games behind the league leaders, a gimmick such as this was one of the few vehicles that Finley had to put fans in the seats for an otherwise meaningless September game. Campaneris actually had minor league experience at virtually every position, including four games as a pitcher early in his minor league career. The plan was for Campaneris to switch positions every inning, culminating with his major league pitching debut in the eighth and an inning behind the plate to end the game. For the first few innings everything went more or less according to plan. Other than committing an error on a routine fly ball in right field, Campaneris handled the spotlight quite well. During his turn on the mound, the opposing California Angels scored a single run off of two walks and a single. He got out of a jam thanks to an unusual double play in which the hitter struck out and Angel star Jim Fregosi was thrown out trying to steal third base. With one out in the ninth the stunt took a dangerous turn when the Angels tried to take advantage of Campaneris' inexperience behind the plate to pull off a double steal of second and home. Campaneris and second baseman Dick Green executed the classic defense against such a play perfectly, with Green cutting off the throw to second and firing back home to Campaneris to try to catch the runner coming in from third. Campaneris was on the losing end of the ensuing collision, which resulted in a shoulder injury that forced him from the game and knocked him out of the lineup for a week. Nevertheless, Campaneris' place in history was secured and Finley had collected quite a few more dollars than he would have from any other September game.

All the speed and defense in the world will not result in a winning team in the absence of a solid pitching staff, and even with the addition of Talbot, the Athletics of 1965 did not feature a solid pitching staff. Orlando Pena, the team's biggest winner on the anemic 1964 staff, lost his first six decisions in 1965 before being relegated to the deepest corner of the bullpen and finally to the Detroit Tigers. Nobody stepped in to fill the void. The team lost 21 of their first 26 games, prompting the dismissal of manager Mel McGaha. His replacement, Haywood Sullivan, was only thirty-four years old and had played for the Athletics as recently as 1963. He fared little better and when the season was over the Athletics were once again mired in last place.

With the recognition that the 1965 season would not be the turnaround year that they had been waiting for, the Athletics looked to their young players to play an increasingly larger role. The shipment of

Rise and Fall

Jim Gentile, hobbled by injuries and a negative attitude, to the Houston Astros in June left the Athletics with the youngest lineup in the major leagues. Among the homegrown players joining the team in 1965, Catfish Hunter earned a spot in the starting pitching rotation in late June and Lew Krausse joined Hunter in the rotation later in the season. Bonus baby Skip Lockwood spent a considerable part of the season on the roster, but his .121 batting average was a sign that he was clearly unable to handle major league pitching. Eight of the pitchers that appeared in Athletic games in 1965 were twenty-two years of age or younger. The young Athletics of 1965 gave an illusion of future hope for Kansas City fans, but the shine only reflected fool's gold; with the exception of Hunter, the vast majority of the Athletics' "Class of '65" would not have a material impact on the club's future success.

Finley, driven by a strong belief that his crop of young talent would one day pave the way toward a winning season, largely stood pat during the winter leading up to 1966. As another sign of Finley's dedication to his prospects, the Athletics traded Jim Landis to the Cleveland Indians in a deal that returned minor leaguer Joe Rudi to the Athletics' family. Finley had signed Rudi to a large bonus in 1964, but a year later Rudi was grabbed by the tribe in the Rule V draft. Finley did not like losing players through the draft and made a habit of trying to recover them whenever possible. Though he was still years away from making an impact at the major league level, Rudi's talents were clearly visible to Finley.

Building and Rebuilding

Like the other Athletic managers before him, Sullivan's managerial career met an early end at Finley's hands. After the 1965 season, Sullivan left the Athletics to begin a long and successful career as a front-office executive for the Boston Red Sox. His replacement for 1966 was former San Francisco Giant manager Alvin Dark. The career National Leaguer's managerial resume was impressive. Upon retiring from an All-Star career as a second baseman he immediately transitioned to the role of skipper of the Giants. Dark enjoyed winning seasons in each of the four years he was there, including the 1962 National League Championship. Though he was successful on the field with the Giants, Dark struggled with controversy off the field. Late in the 1964 season Dark was accused in print of having made disparaging remarks about the Giants' African-American and Hispanic players, an accusation that Dark vehemently denied. His stint at manager ended a short time later when Dark's admission of an extramarital affair with an airline stewardess incited Giant owner Horace Stoneham to show Dark the door. The tumultuous experience with the Giants would serve as excellent preparation for Dark's time with the Athletics. After leaving the Giants, Dark caught on as a coach with the Chicago Cubs, from who Finley recruited Dark as a special assistant late in the 1965 season. Many pundits speculated that Finley recruited Dark in order to secure him as the future successor for the struggling Haywood Sullivan, a prediction that proved to be correct. At 44, Dark fit right in with Finley's patter of hiring young managers (the average age of Dark's predecessors during the Finley era was 41).

Rise and Fall

Youth was clearly the theme of the 1966 Athletics. Of the twenty-six position players to appear for the team in 1966, only two (infielders Ed Charles and Don Blasingame, the latter a member of the team for only four weeks late in the season) were over the age of thirty. The lineup would again feature the steady Dick Green and the exciting Bert Campaneris in the middle of the infield, backed by a cadre of supporting players drawn from the Athletics' developing pool of young talent and from a series of trades pulled off during the season. Perhaps the most important deal was a May trade with the Chicago White Sox that brought utility man Danny Cater to the Athletics. Cater was establishing himself as one of the best pure hitters in the league and would be a valuable member of the Athletics' lineup through the 1969 season. Catfish Hunter served as the team's opening day starter, a tribute to his de facto status as the ace of what appeared to be a very weak pitching staff.

1966 began for the Athletics like every other season in recent memory, with the team in last place. The team lost fourteen of their first seventeen games, a signal that the club's confidence in their stable of youngsters was sadly misplaced. The team wallowed at the very bottom of the standings through Memorial Day and into the first week of June. In the weeks to come the Athletics seemed to stabilize, running off a month of very good baseball that propelled the team into sixth place. By this time the starting pitching staff featured six-foot five-inch rookie arrival Jim Nash. "Jumbo" Jim Nash took the American League by storm by winning twelve out of thirteen decisions in the second half of the season, a performance that earned him recognition as the league's

Building and Rebuilding

Rookie Pitcher of the Year. An eight-game winning streak in September sealed the clubs best finish in years – seventh place in a ten-team league and a .463 winning percentage, a vast improvement over the .364 finish of the previous season. In addition to Nash's twelve victories, Lew Krausse was credited with a career-high fourteen wins. Youngsters Catfish Hunter, Chuck Dobson, Blue Moon Odom, and Paul Linblad rounded out a very promising starting pitching staff. Most impressively, the average age of those six hurlers was *less than twenty-two years old*! The young Athletics' pitching staff was the envy of every major league team, and great things were predicted for the group of young hurlers in the years to come.

The 1966 season also featured the major league debut of September call-ups Sal Bando, the highly touted third baseman considered the heir to that position, and outfielder Rick Monday. In addition to future stars Bando and Monday, September featured a nonstop series of auditions for a promising group of young players that rotated through tryouts in the Athletics' lineup. In a sign of things to come, manager Alvin Dark once used as many as twenty-four players in a single late-season game; player substitutions would become one of the more unusual trademarks of the ballclub in the future.

And so it was that the rebuilding year of 1966 had paid off for the Athletics. For the first time in many years there was genuine cause for optimism within the Athletics' franchise at the conclusion of the baseball season. Great teams are built on great pitching, and Finley had assembled a cast of young pitchers that seemed poised for many years of success. With the continued improvement and maturity of the pitchers and the solid support of a lineup that was also showing signs of jelling, 1967 promised to be a great season for the ballclub.

With an abundance of optimism for the future success of the team, Charlie Finley's master building program had taken a significant leap forward. The pieces were staring to come together, and the years of patient scouting, recruiting, and development of young talent were starting to pay off.

The Setback

On the basis of the exciting conclusion to the 1966 season, the Kansas City Athletics had every reason to expect that their crop of rapidly developing young talent, supported by the quality selections in the Rule IV draft, would lead the Athletics further upward through the American League standings in 1967. Returning manager Alvin Dark's opening day lineup was filled with home grown talent, including Bert Campaneris, Dick Green, sophomore pitching sensation Jim Nash, and rookie outfielder Joe Rudi. Excited by the prospect that the solid 1966 performances by the youthful Athletics would be improved upon in the new season, the Athletics and their fans were geared up for a very successful year. Little did they know that they were in for a major disappointment.

At first, everything went according to the script for the Athletics. Nash picked up where he left off the previous season by winning his opening day start and the team hovered around the .500 mark until mid-June. The high point in the season came on June 18 when an 8-4 win over the Detroit Tigers put the team in fifth place at 31-32, seven games out of first place and in the middle of one of the tightest pennant races in league history. But the team's apparent good fortune turned out to be an illusion.

One of the few disappointments of the season's first three months was pitcher Lew Krausse. Krausse was the son and namesake of an Athletics scout and former Athletics pitcher. As a result of his pedigree and his record-setting signing bonus of $125,000, Lew Krausse was expected to deliver big as a major league pitching star. Krausse's

Rise and Fall

14-9 season in 1966 seemed to indicate that his time had come and great things were expected in 1967. But Krausse struggled out of the gate, losing eleven out of his first fourteen decisions. In sheer frustration after getting shelled in a game on June 6, the drunken Krausse inexplicably fired two rounds from a handgun out of his Kansas City hotel room window. Though the shots did not hit anyone, a police investigation was launched. A cover-up facilitated by owner Charlie Finley spared the Athletics and Krausse the embarrassment of Krausse facing criminal charges. Despite his avoidance of official punishment, Krausse earned a spot deep in Finley's doghouse.

The Krausse incident might have been forgotten had the Athletics continued to perform well as they entered the summer of 1967. But the team's strong play reversed itself in the second half of June. A mid-June five-game losing streak started them on a slide that landed the team just ahead of the last place Washington Senators by the July 4th holiday. A subsequent six-game losing streak placed them squarely in the cellar by the All Star break, a position they were doomed to hold for the duration of the season. While the rest of the American League was fixated on one of the most exciting pennant races imaginable, the Athletics were unraveling.

The Athletics' disappointing season took a decidedly nasty turn beginning on a commercial airline flight after another loss on August 3. As generous as Finley was with his cash as he sought to acquire the player talent that he needed to field a winning team, Finley was equally stingy with expenses that he considered frivolous. Air travel was one of

The Setback

those expenses. Finley could not see the value of transporting his team via a privately owned or chartered air service. Instead, he forced his team to fly on commercial flights, no matter how it might impact their preparedness for a coming series. The August 3 flight from Boston to Kansas City was a perfect example. Not only did the team have to fly on a commercial flight from Boston to Kansas City and play an important series against the Yankees the next day, they had to tolerate not one but two stops along the way. Some of the events that occurred on that flight are agreed to by all parties, while others have never been conclusively resolved and never will be. What is agreed was that the airline stewardesses, some of whom were friendly with the Athletics' players, made the alcohol cart freely available to the players in violation of airline and ballclub policies. From there the story diverges. The Athletic players that took advantage of the opportunity to drown their sorrows over their spiraling record claim that they were a mellow, even somber, well-behaved group of young gentlemen. Other parties claim that they were a group of out of control drunks that offended flight personnel and passengers with their language and behavior. When the conflicting stories reached owner Finley, he chose to believe the latter. Perhaps as a result of both his continuing poor performance and the pistol incident, Finley focused his wrath on Krausse, fining and suspending the pitcher for public drunkenness. He also established a policy that forbade players from drinking during future airline flights and issued a public statement condemning the behavior of his players. The outraged players reacted with a public statement of their own, denying the allegations levied by Finley. It was this public exchange of press releases between players and owner that set the scene for one of the most bizarre series of events in baseball history. Standing at the center of this drama were Finley, manager Dark, and a relatively unknown first baseman named Ken "Hawk" Harrelson.

Prior to August 1967, Ken Harrelson was little more than a footnote in the history of baseball whose primary claim to fame was his irreverent behavior, his progressive wardrobe, and his eccentric lifestyle. Harrelson was a product of the Johnson era of the Athletics, having signed with the team at the age of seventeen in 1959. He joined the club in 1963 and replaced Jim Gentile as the Athletics' starting first baseman in 1965. The arrival of Danny Cater in 1966 made Harrelson expendable and he was dealt to the Washington Senators in June of that year. Almost exactly a year later he was purchased back from the Senators in an attempt to bolster the Athletics' anemic offense. Harrelson was one of the few Athletics performing well at the time of the fateful airplane trip, hitting over .300 in an Athletic uniform since his return. One of the more charismatic and outspoken players on the team's roster, and one of the parties that was smack in the middle of the festivities on the flight in question, Harrelson found himself caught up in the showdown between Finley and his field staff.

The situation reached the critical point when the players' press release became public. Finley called Dark to account for what Finley perceived as the loss of control of the players on the part of Dark, an unforgivable sin in the eyes of Finley. In a bizarre series of events, Finley fired Dark for the crime of losing control of the team. Then, after hearing Dark's sincere and passionate remorse and his similar

The Setback

assessment of the club's potential for future success, Finley reversed the firing and offered Dark a contract extension. Then, upon learning that Dark had lied about his foreknowledge of the players' press release, Finley fired Dark again on the basis that his failure to stop the players' press statement and his subsequent false denial of his foreknowledge of it were acts of disloyalty that Finley could not abide under any circumstances. This time he meant it and Dark stayed fired. Upon hearing of Dark's dismissal, the players considered striking until Dark was reinstated. In the heat of the incident, a reporter asked Ken Harrelson for a statement on the issue. Never at a loss for words, Harrelson spoke his mind. Harrelson's exact words have been lost forever. Harrelson claims to have stated, "The only thing I know is that Charlie Finley's actions of the last few days have been bad for baseball. I think they have been detrimental to the game." In the press, Harrelson was quoted as saying that Finley was "a menace to baseball", a statement that Harrelson vigorously denied. In either case, Harrelson had publicly insulted his boss, and Charlie Finley was not a man who took public insults in stride. Finley demanded a retraction and public apology from Harrelson. Harrelson offered to correct the "menace to baseball" comment because he claimed he was misquoted, but he refused to renounce his other comments. In response, Finley handed Harrelson his unconditional release, the baseball equivalent of firing an employee. Such a move is typically taken only with aging players no longer able to perform at the major league level in the eyes of their owner and rarely if ever with players with any real market value. Perhaps without realizing it, Charlie Finley had created baseball's first modern "free agent".

Rise and Fall

At first Ken Harrelson and indeed the entire baseball world were stunned. Harrelson assumed that there must be a catch, that Finley held some kind of a card that would restrict Harrelson's options or that he would somehow be blackballed from the game. On the contrary, Harrelson went from being an average player, virtually unknown and with no noteworthy achievements on the field, to being baseball's hottest commodity. This was in large part due to the timing. It was Harrelson's good fortune that he was released on August 25. It was the absolute height of the pennant race but still prior to the September 1 freezing of rosters for post-season play. With many teams in the hunt for a championship, the opportunity to pick up a player like Harrelson without having to give up anything other than money in return was VERY appealing for several contending teams. A bidding war for Harrelson's services ensued. The winner was the Boston Red Sox. At the time the Red Sox were in the midst of an unlikely run at the American League Championship. Desperate for an immediate replacement for superstar Tony Conigliaro, critically injured in a famous, near-fatal beaning, the Red Sox offered Harrelson a package totaling the outrageous sum of $150,000. $150,000 for a player that had previously been making $12,000 a year. $150,000 for a player with a lifetime batting average of .238. $150,000 for a player that would hit only .200 for the Red Sox during the stretch drive for the pennant that they eventually won and who hit a miniscule .077 in the subsequent World Series. Not only had Finley created the sport's first true free agent, he had paved the way for the world to see the potential impact on salaries that free agency would potentially deliver. If the owners ever needed confirmation of the

The Setback

importance of the reserve clause to their efforts to contain costs and restrict player salaries, the Ken Harrelson case certainly provided it.

None of this seemed to faze Finley at the time. Satisfied that he had stood by his principles by firing disloyal employees Dark and Harrelson without receiving compensation (which Finley referred to as "blood money" in the case of Harrelson), Finley turned the reigns of the team over to coach Luke Appling and the first base job to Danny Cater and Ramon Webster. In stark contract with the successful conclusion of the 1966 season, the 1967 Athletics finished by losing twenty-three of their final thirty games. Hunter, Krausse, and Nash, three of the pitchers that the Athletics had hoped would lead them to the promised land of the upper tier of the American League, each lost seventeen games. After being selected for the All Star team for the second time in his first three seasons, Hunter ended the season by losing ten of his last fifteen decisions. Nash fell into disfavor with Charlie Finley after a disagreement involving a request by Nash to leave the team before the end of the season to address some personal matters before going off to his annual army reserve assignment. The offense could ill afford the loss of Harrelson and provided virtually no support for the young pitching staff. The only highlights of the season were the presence of the new wave of youngsters that appeared in the lineup throughout the season. The departure of veteran third baseman Ed Charles in May and the relocation of Cater to first base with the departure of Harrelson cleared the way for young Sal Bando to assume the job of starting third baseman in September. Newcomer Reggie Jackson saw time with the club in June before earning a late season spot as the starting right fielder. On

Rise and Fall

September 17 Jackson hit the first of his 563 career home runs. Less conspicuous were the debut of versatile infielder Ted Kubiak and the return of young catcher Dave Duncan, both products of the Athletics' farm system who would play a major role in the future prospects of the ballclub. Duncan was progressing nicely after his brief stint with the team in 1964, developing a batting stroke that resulted in 46 home runs during his time in the California League in 1966.

Never considered more than an interim manager after replacing the fired Alvin Dark, Luke Appling's leadership during the team's nosedive resulted in the ending of his relationship with the Athletics at the conclusion of the season. His replacement would be Bob Kennedy, a veteran baseball man who at forty-seven was older than any of Finley's previous managers with the exception of Appling. In a disappointing contrast to the end of the 1966 season, 1967 had ended on a decidedly sour note. If not for the promise still offered by the youth corps of the Athletics, the team's future potential for success would have looked very bleak indeed.

Goodbye Kansas City, Hello Oakland

Charlie Finley summarized his attitude toward Kansas City with the simple statement, "Kansas City fans are wonderful; there just aren't enough of them." While the Athletics dwelled in the cellar, fans stayed away from the ballpark. The attendance highlight during Finley's Kansas City years came during the club's most successful season of 1966, during which the season attendance topped out at slightly over three quarters of a million fans. But that was not enough to stem the millions of dollars in losses that Finley claimed he was suffering every year. Operating a baseball team is an expensive undertaking, and without the appropriate revenues something had to give. The only thing keeping Finley in Kansas City was the team's lease on Kansas City's Municipal Stadium. By the end of 1967 that lease had expired.

With the expiration of the stadium lease, Finley had three options. One option was to exercise an option to extend the lease. Kansas City officials negotiated with Finley, offering him a package designed to make Kansas City a more financially viable location for the Athletics and hopefully induce Finley to exercise the option. In addition, the city passed a public referendum to secure financing to build brand new stadiums for the Athletics and football's Kansas City Chiefs. Despite the promise of a new stadium and the other incentives, Finley declined to exercise the lease option. If the city were to hold on to their baseball team, it would have to find a way to get rid of Finley. This led to the second alternative – finding a way to get Finley to sell the ballclub to individuals committed to keeping the team in Kansas City. When Finley indicated his unwillingness to exercise his stadium lease option,

Rise and Fall

Kansas City officials attempted to secure a buyer for the club. But after all Finley went through in the 1950's as he tried to buy a baseball team, he was in no hurry to sell out. Finley's asking price was high, too high for any potential buyers.

The final option available to Finley was to move the team to a location that was more economically suited for the franchise. There were two major obstacles in Finley's path. First, he had to find a suitable location; one that offered the prerequisites that Finley believed he needed in order to change his club's financial performance. These prerequisites included a modern stadium, a Finley-friendly local government ready to pave the way through financial incentives, and a suitable fan base to feed the turnstiles. Finley considered a number of alternatives. New Orleans, a city that would continue to be mentioned as a home for the Athletics for as long as Finley was to own the team, was ruled out as the plans for what would later become the Superdome were not sufficiently developed and there was no acceptable interim alternative. The city of Seattle, which was also in the process of constructing a new domed stadium, was also considered. Sicks Stadium, a tiny ballpark that would later become the home for the ill-fated Seattle Pilots, was available as a short-term option until Seattle's Kingdome was ready. The city of Milwaukee also wooed Finley. Milwaukee had lost the Braves to Atlanta a few years earlier and was eager to bring baseball back to the city. Finally, there was Oakland. Oakland had a long history as a minor league city. The city had just completed the construction of the Oakland-Alameda County Coliseum in 1966 as the new home for the Oakland Raiders football team and had hoped to use the new facility as a tool to draw Major League

Goodbye Kansas City, Hello Oakland

Baseball. The only potential drawback to Oakland was the close proximity of the San Francisco Giants, just across the bay from Oakland. Unlike Seattle and New Orleans, each a virgin territory for Major League Baseball, Finley would have to share at least part of his potential fan base with another team. Despite this, in the end Finley chose Oakland as the new home for his team.

Finley's decision to move the Athletics to Oakland for the 1968 season led to the second obstacle – securing American League permission to move the team. Franchise owners are not at liberty to move their teams wherever or whenever they like. All transactions involving baseball teams, including the sale or relocation of a team, are subject to the approval of the other league owners. The American League was heavily pressured by Kansas City and Missouri political leaders to protect their franchise, but in the end the league decided that they had little recourse but to allow Finley to move the team. As a compromise, the American League agreed to expand for the 1969 season and to offer Kansas City-based investors the first rights to one of the new expansion teams. The proposal was accepted and the Kansas City Royals were eventually born. Kansas City had simultaneously guaranteed the future of Major League Baseball in their community and rid themselves of the now despised Finley. For his part, Finley now had a clear path to what he trusted would be the more lucrative Bay Area.

Rise and Fall

The people of Oakland greeted their new ballclub with open arms. Once again, there just "weren't enough of them". The competition from nearby San Francisco likely depressed attendance. For decades following the Athletics' move to the area, a debate raged regarding whether or not the area could sustain two Major League Baseball teams. Attendance at the Giants' Candlestick Park also declined significantly when the Athletics arrived. Despite the novelty of having a brand new major league team in the area, the Athletics' attendance was still among the worst in the American League. And the Athletics were no longer cellar dwellers. Adding insult to injury, when the brand new Kansas City Royals made their debut in 1969, playing in the very same stadium abandoned by Finley two years earlier, they outdrew the superior-playing Athletics. When Royals Stadium finally opened in 1972, attendance almost doubled to well over one million fans, despite the fact that the Royals were not serious contenders in the American League western division. This was no fluke, as the Royals consistently drew over a million fans every year. In contrast, the Athletics barely topped the one million mark only twice in the seventies (in 1973 and 1975), despite being the dominant team in the game of baseball through much of that time. The disparity in attendance reached its peak in 1979 when the Royals drew over two and a quarter million fans while the Athletics drew an embarrassing three hundred thousand, a differential of 700%.

Goodbye Kansas City, Hello Oakland

And so it was that Oakland was not the financial paradise that Charlie Finley had hoped for when he moved his team there for the start of the 1968 season.

Nevertheless, it would be the site for one of the most incredible climbs from the basement to the top of the standings in the history of sports.

Perfection On The Road To Respectability

Rookie manager Bob Kennedy's opening day lineup for the Athletics' inaugural season in Oakland featured four players that would figure prominently in their future success. Catfish Hunter had regained the mantle of ace of what was by all accounts a shaky pitching staff and was given the honor of performing as the opening day starter for the second time in his short career. Joining Bert Campaneris in the staring lineup that day were third baseman Sal Bando and right fielder Reggie Jackson. The placement of Bando and Jackson in the regular lineup further emphasized the team's ongoing commitment to providing opportunities for their homegrown talent. Both players had starred in the legendary Arizona State University baseball program prior to joining the Athletics. Both had driven the fast track to major leaguer status. Both had struggled at the plate in limited duty with the Athletics in 1967, with Bando hitting just .192 and Jackson coming in even lower at .178. But Kennedy and the Athletics could see the potential in both players and both became every day fixtures in the A's lineup. Dick Green remained on the roster, but had temporarily lost his starting second base job to John Donaldson. Another key player on the roster was Rick Monday, who by this time was comfortably ensconced as the every day center fielder. The Athletics added catcher Dave Duncan and outfielder Joe Rudi to the roster as the season progressed, with the former showing big league power when he took over as the starting catcher for the injured Jim Pagliaroni during the middle part of the season. Rudi held the starting left field position for several weeks before receding into a backup role later in the season.

Perfection On The Road To Respectability

One of the most notable new faces in an Athletic uniform as the 1968 season began played no position on the field, despite being voted baseball's greatest living player just a year later. He was Joe DiMaggio, and Charlie Finley scored a great coup by signing the retired Yankee Clipper as a present to the hometown bay area fans. DiMaggio's role as a special coach came with lots of strings attached (for example, no coaching on the baselines – ever!), but it was worth it for two reasons. The first was economic – DiMaggio was revered in the bay area as much as he was in New York. And perhaps more importantly, DiMaggio's presence was a godsend to several of the Athletics' players. Young Joe Rudi became a special project of DiMaggio's, and Rudi credited his coach for making him one of the very finest outfielders of the 1970's.

1968 went down in history as "the year of the pitcher", a season in which pitching dominated baseball like never before. Overall, the performance of the Athletics' pitching staff was a vast improvement over anything achieved by their Kansas City predecessors. Though there was still immense room for improvement, the young pitching staff was clearly on the rise, with Lew Krausse, Chuck Dobson, Catfish Hunter, Jim Nash, and Blue Moon Odom all winning ten or more games.

The Athletics had a five game losing streak in April, a six game losing streak in May, a seven game losing streak in June / July, and another five game losing streak in August. These streaks prevented the team from gaining enough traction to truly advance in the standings, particularly in light of the fact that the team was not able to cobble together a winning streak of more than four games. Despite this, the

Rise and Fall

team stayed within a few games of the .500 mark almost the entire season, ending two games above .500 at 82-80. It was the first time since the 1952 season that the franchise had enjoyed a winning season, and after the debacles of the Kansas City years winning more than half of their games was the turning point that Charlie Finley had been waiting for and relentlessly building toward. This moral victory was offset very slightly by the fact that the team, by finishing in sixth place, still had not cracked the top half of the league standings. Despite this disappointment, there were many causes for optimism for the future.

The real progress for the Athletics came at the plate. In a year where outstanding offensive performances were rare, several Athletic hitters were beginning to make a name for themselves. Only two American League hitters ended with a batting average of .290 or better – league leader Carl Yastrzemski (.301) and Athletic Danny Cater (.290). Bert Campaneris led the league both in hits and in stolen bases; his 62 steals were 22 more than his nearest rival. In addition, Reggie Jackson's name appeared for the first time among the top sluggers in the league, as his 29 home runs were good enough for fourth in the league. For the first time in recent history, the Athletic lineup had the strength and depth to cause concern for opposing pitchers.

An important event in the evolution of the Athletics' dynasty took place at the end of the 1968 season. After winning the starting third base job in spring training, Sal Bando proceeded to quickly transition from a raw rookie to an every day player to captain of the Oakland Athletics. Displaying maturity far beyond his twenty-four years, Bando

Perfection On The Road To Respectability

led by example and soon became a leader on the field and in the clubhouse. Even though he had yet to display the offensive ability that would one day earn him the recognition as the top offensive third baseman in the American League, Bando nevertheless became an indispensable asset within the Athletics' lineup. When the season ended, Bando had appeared in every one of the team's games, a feat he would repeat the following season. As Bando's influence on the ballclub grew, it soon became impossible to think of the Athletics without thinking of Bando. "Captain Sal" soon became a symbol of the Oakland Athletics.

Viewed in its entirety, the 1968 season was a major milestone in the Athletics' march toward respectability. But it was a seemingly ordinary evening in early May that provided the most unmistakable evidence that a very special story was developing in Oakland.

Although Catfish Hunter had turned twenty-two only a couple of days prior to the start of the 1968 season, he was already an experienced major league pitcher with almost one hundred games under his belt when the season began. His reputation in his early years was that of a very consistent, solid performer with a predisposition to give up the long ball. Hunter was not overpowering like many of the great pitchers of the day; instead, he delivered what hitters referred to as a "comfortable 0-for-4". Though his career record at that time was below .500, Hunter's talent had been recognized to the point where he was named to the American League All-Star team in 1966 and 1967. By 1968 he was still a .500

Rise and Fall

pitcher, but was also clearly honing the skills that would eventually take him to the Hall of Fame. On April 27 he pitched six and two-thirds innings of no-hit ball against the California Angels before he tired and yielded his first hit.

On the cool spring evening of May 8, Hunter's record stood at 2-2. His opponent for the six o'clock, twilight start was the hard-hitting Minnesota Twins. In a league dominated by pitching, the Twin lineup featured many of the top hitters in the American League, including future Hall of Famers Rod Carew and Harmon Killebrew and hitting stars Bob Allison and Tony Oliva. For Hunter the night began with a minor controversy. Like many pitchers, Hunter took great pride in his hitting. Hunter was able to help himself at the plate, but manager Bob Kennedy did not like his pitchers taking batting practice on days when they were scheduled to start and he angrily ejected Hunter from the batting cage prior to the game. The confrontation was a distraction that could seriously rattle a young pitcher, but Hunter refocused on his primary task at hand – shutting down the Twins lineup. Hunter took his position on the pitching mound in front of a meager crowd of a little over six thousand fans. Little did they know that they were about to witness an historic event, one that would be a turning point in the Athletics' fortunes.

For Hunter, the game progressed through the early innings without a hitch. One by one the mighty Twins hitters were retired. Through the first five innings, not a single Twin hitter reached base. Though not a strikeout pitcher, Hunter fanned five of the first fifteen

Perfection On The Road To Respectability

hitters he faced, two of them on called third strikes. In the sixth he added to this total by striking out the side. The Athletics' players took notice of the fact that Hunter had not allowed a base runner and initiated an odd ritual as old as the game of baseball – when a pitcher has a no-hitter going in the late innings, nobody on the bench speaks to them, lest they jinx their masterpiece. There were now only two major hurdles for Hunter to overcome in order to achieve baseball immortality – he had to get through the dangerous Twin lineup one more time, and his team needed to score a run; as great as Hunter had been in the first six innings, his opponent, Dave Boswell, had also kept the Athletics from scoring. A 0-0 pitcher's dual was not uncommon in "the year of the pitcher"; if the Athletics did not score soon the pressure on Hunter would be increased.

Hunter held his end of the bargain in the top of the seventh, retiring the dangerous Cesar Tovar and Rod Carew before striking out Harmon Killebrew. Hunter came to the plate in the bottom of the inning with a runner on third and one out. He laid down a perfect bunt, beating it out for a hit and driving in the first run of the game. With six hitters to go, Catfish Hunter now had a perfect game within reach and a lead on the scoreboard.

The middle of the Twins lineup was as good or better than the middle of any lineup in the game. Still, Hunter retired Tony Oliva, Ted Uhlaender, and Bob Allison in the eighth without incident. In the bottom of the eighth Hunter capped off an Athletic rally by driving in two more runs with his third hit of the day. He entered the top of the ninth with a three-for-four night at the plate, with three runs batted in, a 4-0 lead, and only three outs to go to immortality.

The first hitter for the Twins in the ninth inning was scheduled to be Jackie Hernandez, the weakest link in the Twin lineup. Twins manager Cal Ermer wanted Hunter to earn his perfect game, and he sent the veteran John Roseboro up to hit for Hernandez. Roseboro grounded to second for the first out. Catcher Bruce Look fanned on a called strike for the second out and Hunter's tenth strikeout. Rich Reese, one of the best pinch hitters in the game, was sent to the plate to break up the perfect game. Hunter went to 2-2 on Reese before throwing Reese a slider which Hunter later claimed "cut the plate in half" but which was called a ball. With a 3-2 count, Reese proceeded to build the tension by fouling off the next five pitches. Reese swung and missed at the sixth and Hunter had his perfect game. It was the first regular-season perfect game in the American League in over sixty years and it further elevated Hunter's status as one of the games up-and-coming stars. The giddy Finley gave Hunter a $5,000 bonus on the spot, and the repentant Kennedy told Hunter that he could take batting practice whenever he wanted. Catfish Hunter was on the top of the baseball world. In a bitter twist of fate, his next mound appearance would again be against those same Twins, this time on their home turf. In stark contrast to the night of May 8, Rod Carew led off the bottom of the first with a home run. This was followed by a walk, another home run, another walk, and another home run. Hunter had gone from retiring all twenty-seven Twin hitters to getting shelled in the first inning by the same team just a week later.

Perfection On The Road To Respectability

Catfish Hunter's perfect game on May 8, 1968 and the continued development of Jackson, Bando, Campaneris, and Monday sent a signal to the American League fraternity – Finley's investment in his youth program was beginning to pay huge dividends and the Oakland Athletics were from this point forward to be taken very, very seriously.

As the Athletics looked eagerly ahead to improving upon their 1968 performance, there was one potentially significant hurdle that they had to clear as they prepared for the 1969 season. The second expansion in American league history would introduce two new ball clubs for the 1969 season, an event that necessitated a special draft to provide the new teams with talent for their inaugural seasons. Each existing team was to submit a list of "protected" players that would be exempt from the draft, with the remainder available in the multi-round draft. Each team underwent the difficult choice of deciding which players to protect. Difficult choices between protecting established players, high potential minor leaguers, or other potentially key players had to be made. Poor choices could have the effect of setting the Athletics' progress back a number of years and delaying their march toward excellence. In retrospect the draft proved to be a minor inconvenience, potentially benefiting the club by clearing out veterans that blocked the progress of rookies as well as weeding out a few prospects that ultimately had little place in the evolving picture of the future. In the draft the Athletics lost veteran relief pitchers Jack Aker and Diego Segui, clearing the path for the arrival of future Hall of Famer Rollie Fingers. Joe Keough and Skip

Rise and Fall

Lockwood, both of who were once highly-regarded prospects but neither of whom fit in with the Athletics' current plans, were also selected, as were veteran Jim Gosger and minor leaguer Don O'Riley. If anything, the 1968 expansion draft helped the Athletics rather than hinder them. The team was ready to step up to the next level.

Priming the Engine

Not even a .500 season could save Bob Kennedy from Charlie Finley's managerial revolving door. The most successful manager in recent franchise history was fired immediately after the 1968 season. Hank Bauer, who managed 264 games for Finley's Kansas City Athletics in the early 1960's, a few games short of Alvin Dark's record as the longest serving manager during the Finley era, was rehired by Finley to manage the team in 1969. Amidst the high expectations set by the Athletics of 1968, the 1969 team set about the task of moving into the top tier of the American League elite. Fortunately for the Athletics, a milestone event in the history of baseball would make that journey a little easier.

Since the birth of both the American and National Leagues, each league had been organized as a single unit, with the team that won the most games during the course of the season being recognized as the League Champion and a participant in the season's World Series. This arrangement worked well through the decades in which there were only eight teams in each league. In 1961 the American League expanded to ten teams and the National League followed suit a year later. The climb to the top of the league's standings was now more difficult. A plan to further expand each league to twelve teams for the 1969 season compounded this issue. In the face of raging concern that a twelve-team league would limit the ability of the majority of franchises to reach the post-season, and over the furious objections of baseball traditionalists, both leagues agreed to split their teams into eastern and western divisions for 1969. Based upon the geographical locations of each of the

Rise and Fall

American League franchises, the Athletics would be joined in the new western division by the California Angels, Chicago White Sox, Minnesota Twins, and the brand new, expansion Kansas City Royals and Seattle Pilots. This split proved to be a stroke of good fortunate for the Athletics. As expansion teams, the Royals and Pilots were not expected to be a competitive threat in the foreseeable future. Of the remaining four teams, all had finished 1968 in the bottom half of the standings, with the Athletics at the top of that list in sixth place. Teams aligned with the new eastern division had won thirty-five of the last thirty-seven American League Championships, with the 1959 victory of the White Sox and the 1965 triumph of the Twins standing as the lone exceptions. The baseball gods were clearly smiling on the Athletics when the divisional map was drawn.

On paper the Athletics' 1969 opening day lineup looked very similar to that of the previous season. Sal Bando, Reggie Jackson, Bert Campaneris, Rick Monday, and Danny Cater, all holdovers from the previous season, returned to their position as regulars in what was becoming a very potent offensive lineup. Dick Green had reclaimed his starting role as the team's second baseman and rookie catcher Dave Duncan joined the club as part of what would become a rotation of catchers over the next few seasons. Though the bench was arguably thin, the core of the lineup featured players that would become the game's top stars of the 1970's.

The pitching staff was again built upon a nucleus of young, developing arms. Few teams could boast three starters as effective as the

Priming the Engine

Athletics' top three of Chuck Dobson, Catfish Hunter, and Blue Moon Odom. The problem facing the Athletics as the season progressed was supporting the three aces with viable fourth and fifth starters and a reliable bullpen. The seeds of an effective supporting cast were sown by the likes of swingman Rollie Fingers, who switched back and forth between the starting rotation and the bullpen as needs dictated, and by Paul Linblad, who had quietly established himself as a solid left-handed reliever.

The scene for the 1969 western division championship race was set in early April when the Minnesota Twins reeled off a seven game winning streak, followed in short order by an eight game winning streak. The Twins were experiencing a collective resurgence, four seasons after winning the American League Championship and coming within a game of taking home the World Championship before being shut down in Game 7 of the 1965 World Series by the great Sandy Koufax. The potent lineup against which Catfish Hunter had thrown his perfect game just one year earlier had grown even stronger and was now supported by brash rookie manager Billy Martin and a strong pitching staff. In contrast to the youthful, homegrown Athletics, the Twins' roster was peppered with seasoned veterans, some dating back to the franchise's days in Washington as the original Washington Senators, and others that had been acquired in trades or through the minor league draft.

The Athletics countered the Twins' surge with a seven game winning streak of their own in early May. By the 16th of the month the Athletics had moved into sole possession of first place, a game ahead of the Twins. At that point the team's fortunes changed as they suffered five consecutive losses by one run. The Athletics recovered to stay within striking distance of the first-place Twins, and by mid-June the club was again at the top of the divisional standings. The upstart Athletics held the lead going into the July 4 holiday, buoyed by the old baseball adage that the team that leads the standings on that date is favored to win the championship at season's end. A three game sweep of the Athletics at the hands of the Twins on July 4-6 flipped the two front-runners in the standings. The Twins rode a streak of eighteen wins in twenty games to a five game lead over the second place Athletics. Again the Athletics recovered enough to stay within striking distance of the division-leading Twins through the month of August. As late as August 26 the Athletics were just two games behind the Twins.

Beginning in 1969 and throughout their domination of the American League western division, the Athletics left no stone unturned when it came to rounding out their roster with valuable role players when the pennant race heated up. According to the rules of the day, June 15 was the last date on which teams had the unrestricted right to make player transactions with other teams. The June 15 "trading deadline" was established in 1923 to protect against wealthy teams padding their roster deep into the season in order to gain an unfair pennant race advantage over less fortunate teams. In order to move a player from one team to another after that deadline, the club that owns the player in question must ask for permission, known as a "waiver", to make the transaction. Permission is granted by publishing the named player through the Major League Baseball offices on what was referred to as the "waiver list". *The Sporting News* once called the waiver list "baseball's classified advertising section". The other major league teams have the right to claim any player put forward in this manner. If a team chooses not to claim a player they are said to have "waived" their right to claim the player. For this reason, this process of clearing a player for a trade is referred to as "asking waivers". If another team does not claim a player, the player can be moved without restriction. If a player is claimed by a team, the original team can sell the player to the claiming team for a modest "waiver price", negotiate a trade for the player, or remove the player from the waiver list. If multiple teams claim a player, the teams with the worst record have the first option to acquire the player. This process is repeated constantly after the training deadline as teams maneuver to move unwanted players from their roster or add a late season acquisition to fill a vital role for a pennant drive. During the pennant races of 1969-1976, the Athletics were frequent users of the waiver process. The A's waiver class of 1969 featured Bob Johnson, Tito Francona, and Juan Pizzaro, acquired in July, August, and September, respectively. Johnson and Francona were among the game's top pinch hitters, forming a righty / lefty combination that added significant punch to the Athletics' bench. During their short time with the team in 1969, Johnson and Francona hit a remarkable .343 and .341 respectively, mostly as pinch hitters. Pizzaro joined very late in the season to give the Athletics a much-needed left arm in the starting rotation. All three players were emblematic of the type of player that would be acquired by the Athletics after the trading deadline in the coming years – quality players, too far past their prime to make an

Rise and Fall

impact with their current clubs but who could immediately fill a specific gap in the Athletics' attack.

Despite the addition of Johnson and Francona, the Athletics fell apart after their high water mark of August 26, going only 15-22 the remainder of the way. Charlie Finley, frantic over the self-destruction of the team, fired Hank Bauer on September 16 and replaced him with John McNamara. It was too late to make a difference. The A's final record of 88-74 was good enough for a second place finish, nine games behind the divisional champion Twins and seventeen games ahead of the third place Angels. The second place finish was the highest placement for the franchise since the salad days of 1932. But second place was not good enough.

In addition to the emergence of the Athletics as a legitimate pennant contender, the other big news in Oakland in 1969 was the development of Reggie Jackson into one of the premier sluggers in the game. The highlight of Jackson's season was his quest to break the single season home run record. In reaction to the steady offensive decline culminating in the worst offensive year in baseball history in 1968, Major League Baseball attempted to recalibrate the game to take away some of the factors that facilitated the domination of the pitcher, including lowering the pitching mound for the 1969 season. These adjustments combined with the watering down of pitching talent due to the recent expansion to bring about a resurgence of the home run in the national game. The rebirth of the slugger in the American League was illustrated by what appeared at mid-season to be a serious challenge of Roger Maris' record of sixty-one home runs by not one but two sluggers – Jackson and Frank Howard of the Washington Senators. By August, Jackson was the major league home run leader. Jackson hit home run number forty-one on August 2, his team's 101st game. If he could maintain that pace, Jackson would break the Maris record with room to spare. But he could not maintain the pace. From that point forward, Jackson managed only six more home runs and finished third in the home run race to Harmon Killebrew and Frank Howard. Despite the disappointment of missing the record, Jackson had announced to the world that he was a force to be reckoned with, and for the rest of his time in Oakland his bat would be the single most potent weapon in the Athletics' lineup.

The emergence of Jackson was not the only major development by Athletics' personnel. Outfielder Joe Rudi rejoined the club to stay in September, earning a starting spot in the outfield that would largely remain his for the next seven seasons. Third baseman Sal Bando also blossomed into a star, raising his home run total from nine in his first full season to a career high of thirty-one in 1969, good enough to earn for him an All Star berth. In addition, Bert Campaneris repeated his career high total of sixty-two stolen bases and Rick Monday, Dick Green, and Danny Cater provided strong offensive contributions. Although the catcher's spot was problematic, Dave Duncan and September call-up Gene Tenace provided hope for the future. The pitching staff was led by Blue Moon Odom and Chuck Dobson, with fifteen wins apiece, and

Rise and Fall

Catfish Hunter, who provided an additional twelve. Rollie Fingers earned his first twelve major league saves to lead the bullpen. Unbeknownst to the baseball world at the time, the most significant development on the Athletics' pitching staff for 1969 was the July 20 debut of nineteen year-old southpaw Vida Blue. In keeping with the Athletics' tradition of rushing their young talent to the major leagues, Blue joined the team after only a season and a half in the minors. A disastrous start only served to delay Blue's development – he would be heard from again.

The disappointment of the late season collapse of the Athletics in 1969 fueled Finley's desire to complete the puzzle that would comprise a championship team. With Minnesota clearly the leaders of a weak American League western division, Finley went shopping during the post-season to try to fill in the missing pieces.

By 1970 the Athletics had arguably the best young nucleus in the American League, if not in all of baseball. Dick Green, Bert Campaneris, and Sal Bando, though not of the same superstar caliber of Connie Mack's $100,000 Infield so many decades before, formed a very solid unit. Although Danny Cater had provided steady offensive support at first base since his acquisition in 1966, he was the quintessential line drive hitter, and first base is predominantly a power position. The Athletics felt that more offense was required at first base if the team was to move to a higher level. Left field was also a problem. Rick Monday

Priming the Engine

and Reggie Jackson gave the Athletics two-thirds of an outstanding outfield, but the rotation of left fielders in the prior two seasons did not provide the necessary third leg. Joe Rudi's lack of offense in prior trials had eroded confidence in his readiness to play every day. A new left fielder would be needed. In addition, the revolving door behind home plate would need to be addressed. Lastly, the starting rotation urgently required a reliable left-hander and the bullpen required another stopper to support the young Rollie Fingers. These needs formed the basis for Charlie Finley's shopping list in the weeks following the conclusion of the 1969 season. True to form, Finley was successful in filling every order. First Finley dealt the disappointing Jim Nash to the Atlanta Braves for veteran left fielder Felipe Alou. Nash had failed to meet the high expectations set during his sensational run as a rookie phenom in 1966, and had most recently drawn attention to himself by ballooning up to 245 pounds. Next, Finley turned to the New York Yankees, with whom he had announced a trade embargo just a few years before. From the Yankees, Finley acquired catcher Frank Fernandez and lefty pitcher Al Downing. To further beef up his pitching staff, Finley acquired Jim "Mudcat" Grant from the St. Louis Cardinals and reacquired Diego Segui from the Seattle Pilots. For Segui this would be his third tour of duty with Finley and the Athletics. All of these transactions took place during a four-day spree in December. Finley took a month off from the trade mart before making his next move, the acquisition of slugging first baseman Don Mincher from the Pilots for a package that included Lew Krausse, who like Nash was a major disappointment after a promising start to his career. Once seen as the cornerstone for the Athletics' building program, Krausse's nine-year career with the A's organization had peaked with his fourteen win season in 1966 and bottomed out with his role in the firing of Alvin Dark in 1967. Though he would go on to pitch for five more seasons with four different teams, Lew Krausse would no longer be a factor on the major league scene.

Finley had now plugged each of the holes in the 1969 team. John McNamara, back to pilot the Athletics for his first full season, would have no excuse for not delivering the pennant lest he suffer the same fate as Bauer and those who preceded him.

But it was not the Athletics' year.

The problems started in spring training. Reggie Jackson, on the heels of his remarkable 1969 season, wanted to triple his salary from $20,000 to $60,000. Finley, bitterly disappointed in Jackson's late season fade and the resulting impact on the club's aborted pennant hopes, would not offer more that $40,000. Finley justified his position by criticizing Jackson's late season fade in 1969, publicly questioning Jackson's ability to perform under pressure (a charge that Finley would later have cause to regret as Jackson grew to earn the moniker "Mr. October" for his clutch post-season performances in the 1970's). With little recourse, Jackson eventually gave in, but the bitterness of the contract dispute and Finley's hard-nosed negotiation style had a long-term impact on Jackson's relationship with Finley and negatively impacted Jackson's performance on the field. Jackson's batting average was well below .200 into June and his power numbers dropped significantly. Downing suffered from the recurrence of serious arm

Priming the Engine

troubles that had made him expendable by the Yankees, Alou proved to be a major disappointment at the plate, and the previously reliable Dick Green's offensive contribution was virtually zero. At the same time the Twins leapt to the front of the pack by winning eight of their first ten games while the Athletics stumbled out of the gate. A five game losing streak at the close of April left the Athletics five games behind the Twins and the upstart California Angels. While the Athletics struggled to find a rhythm, the Twins won games at a pace of over .700. At the beginning of June the Athletics stood eight games behind the Twins. In June the Athletics tried to jump-start their struggling offense with the waiver acquisition of Tommy Davis. The club cut into the Twins lead in June, but a disastrous July put them eleven games back in third place on July 20. It was at this point that the Athletics caught fire, winning ten of eleven games to move ahead of the Angels into second place, seven games behind the Twins. Their strong play continued, and they cut the Twins lead to four games on August 14. Then the bottom fell out. The Athletics lost ten of the next eleven games, dropping the team back into third place and ending their hopes for a first-place finish. The club rallied one last time, winning ten of eleven once again from August 28 through September 7. The red-hot Athletics rolled into Minnesota for a three game series with the front-runners on the 9th, trailing the Twins by only five and a half games. They proceeded to be swept, effectively eliminating them from pennant contention. Finley raised the white flag of surrender in mid-September, trading veteran bullpen ace Mudcat Grant to the Pittsburgh Pirates for minor leaguer Angel Mangual, following that two days later by selling Tommy Davis to the Chicago Cubs. At the time the Pirates and Cubs were embroiled in an intense

Rise and Fall

three-way battle with the New York Mets for first place in the National League eastern division. Met fans were understandably furious that their two main rivals were given a late-season boost by Finley, but Finley wanted to clean house and receive the maximum value for the two veterans. It would not be the last time that Finley would attempt to cut his losses late in a season by sending impact players to pennant contenders, but in subsequent years it would be Finley that would usually prosper on the receiving end of similar transactions.

For the second season in a row, the Athletics seemed to fall just a bit short of the talent required to take the divisional crown. Coming so close without ultimate success for the second year in a row was bitterly disappointing for Finley and his ballplayers. But the disappointment of losing the divisional race for the second consecutive season would be partially offset by an amazing story that was to develop on the pitcher's mound.

After his disappointing 1969 major league debut, Vida Blue was sent to AAA Iowa to begin the 1970 season. Recalled in September, he was again hit hard in his first start. His next start was in Kansas City September 11, one day after the disastrous sweep by the Twins. This time Blue took a no-hitter into the eighth inning when a two-out single by Pat Kelly resulted in the only hit the Royals would register that night. Blue had made a splash, but it was only a drop in the bucket compared to what would come next. After another shaky start, Blue was given the task of starting against the mighty Twins lineup on September 21. On that night Blue was unhittable, just as Catfish Hunter had been against

Priming the Engine

those same Twins two years earlier. The only Twin to reach base that night was Harmon Killebrew, the recipient of a fourth inning walk. The Twins claimed the divisional prize, but Blue's no-hitter over their main nemesis provided a shot in the arm for the Athletics that would carry over into the next season.

In addition to Blue's emergence, there were numerous other bright notes in the Athletics' 1970 performance. Catfish Hunter's continued development yielded his first winning season and an 18-14 record. More notably, Hunter's reputation as a workhorse was further established by his forty starts, a total matched by fellow starter Chuck Dobson. Dobson contributed sixteen victories, while Mudcat Grant anchored the bullpen before being traded in September. Joe Rudi matured offensively and hit for a sizzling .309 average while continuing to display his developing defensive skills. Catchers Dave Duncan and Gene Tenace both delivered solid performances in limited duty, eventually costing Frank Fernandez his starting catcher's job in August.

No degree of euphoria resulting from Blue's late season masterpiece and the evolution of the other young Athletics' talent could save McNamara's job. When the dust settled and the season ended, the Athletics had won a single game more than they had the previous season and had finished the same nine games behind the same first place Twins. McNamara suffered the same fate as every other manager who had disappointed the Athletics' owner – termination. In his place for the 1971 season would be Dick Williams, the turn around artist that had guided the 1967 Boston Red Sox to their unlikely "impossible dream"

Rise and Fall

League Championship in 1967. Though the Red Sox had been an annual disappointment in the three seasons following their miraculous victory, Williams was considered to be an excellent choice to manage the Athletics. Like Bauer and Dark he had a proven track record of winning, and like so many of his predecessors he was still a very young man by managerial standards. But Williams was no fool; he knew his mission was to capture first place and there would likely be no tolerance for second best on the part of Finley. Taking the Athletics those final nine games would require luck, skill, and fulfillment of the promise shown by Charlie Finley's cast of home grown talent.

Dress Rehearsal

In a departure from prior off seasons, the Athletics stood idle during the 1970-1971 hot stove season and refrained from making any major player moves. For Dick Williams to close the gap between second and first place he would have to do it with the lineup that was in place at the end of the disappointing 1970 season. The club survived a scare when veteran second baseman Dick Green announced his retirement, the initiation of what would become an almost annual event for the second baseman. Green cited the rigors of travel and the desire to spend time with his family as his reasons for prematurely leaving the sport. The club frantically but unsuccessfully canvassed other teams in an attempt to land a replacement for Green, although they did come close to acquiring Red Sox second baseman Mike Andrews. Ironically, Andrews would have a major impact on Athletics' history two years later. It finally took the intercession of Charlie Finley to coax the reluctant Green back for another season.

There were two primary differences between the Athletics of 1970 and their 1971 counterparts. A subtle difference was the additional year of seasoning and experience garnered by the homegrown Athletic players. Dave Duncan, Joe Rudi, Rollie Fingers, Vida Blue, and indeed even Sal Bando, Catfish Hunter, and Reggie Jackson, benefited from an additional year of experience and came into the 1971 season more prepared than ever to compete at the highest level. A more visible difference was in the quality of the bench. While the 1970 club had entered that season with a well-stocked bench featuring a healthy mixture of solid veterans and up-and-coming youngsters, the 1971 team faced opening day with a very thin supporting cast that put additional pressure on the starting team to perform. Finley reacquired Tommy Davis, sold to the Chicago Cubs the previous September, to provide some additional depth on the bench, but Davis alone could not provide the bench strength necessary for a championship. Compounding the team's lack of depth, both Blue Moon Odom and Chuck Dobson began the season on the disabled list, forcing Williams to utilize relief specialists Fingers and Diego Segui in the starting rotation.

The 1971 season started badly with losses in the first three games, with opening day starter Vida Blue unable to get through the second inning against the perennially weak Washington Senators. In desperation the Athletics further depleted their bench by sending Felipe Alou to the Yankees in return for two second-tier pitchers in an attempt to beef up the thin pitching staff. Mother Nature interceded in the fourth game of the season as Blue shut out the Royals in six rain-shortened innings for his and the team's first win of the season. The team then went on to reel off a span of fourteen wins in sixteen games. The Athletics took over sole possession of first place on April 16, determined to hold on to that prize no matter what it took. By the end of April the club had built up an early four game lead over their nearest rival.

The early days of the season brought signs that if the Athletics were ever going to make a run for the pennant, 1971 was the year to do it. Minnesota, the dominant powerhouse of the western division for the first two years of divisional play, was suffering from the onset of age and injury that significantly detracted from their performance. None of the

Dress Rehearsal

remaining teams seemed poised to assume the role of heir to the Twins, leaving the field largely clear for the Athletics.

The Athletics were still holding their lead in the second week of May when they engineered a trade with the Senators in which they dealt Don Mincher, Paul Linblad, and Frank Fernandez for first baseman Mike Epstein and lefty reliever Darold Knowles. They followed that deal with the acquisition of the versatile Curt Blefary and first baseman Mike Hegan. These new additions, in combination with rookie Angel Mangual, provided the bench depth that the club so desperately needed. Better still, Dobson and Odom returned to full duty in May to round out the pitching staff.

But the real story of the first weeks of the 1971 season was the meteoric rise of Vida Blue. Though the Athletics had a taste of the young left-hander's talents with his late season no-hitter the previous September, nobody could have accurately predicted how dominant Blue would be in his first full season. After his disastrous opening day performance, Blue reeled off a streak of ten consecutive victories. The ten victories all featured complete game performances by Blue and included five shutouts. With his tenth victory on May 23, Blue had reduced his ERA to a microscopic 1.03 in addition to establishing himself as the major league strikeout leader. All of baseball became inflicted with Blue Fever as the outstanding young pitcher dominated hitters and headlines. Everywhere Blue pitched, attendance skyrocketed as baseball fans around the country clamored to see the young phenom. In addition to Blue's amazing performance, Catfish Hunter also caught

Rise and Fall

fire. After losing his first two starts, Hunter reeled off victories in eight consecutive starts. Though not the dominant personal presence that the powerful and charismatic Blue enjoyed, Hunter had clearly matured as a pitcher and was making good the promise he had demonstrated way back in 1964.

The Athletics continued to dominate the competition through Memorial Day and into the month of June. By the end of June the Athletics had opened up a double-digit lead over the field and with consistently strong performances by starters Blue, Hunter, and the now healthy Dobson, losing streaks were not a concern. Blue continued to sizzle into the summer, winning his nineteenth game on July 27. Although Hunter had cooled slightly, Dobson picked up the slack by winning his first nine decisions. Offensively, the Athletics were strong enough to provide just the right level of support for the pitching staff. Though Jackson was still not showing the dominant power he had demonstrated in the first half of 1969, he did show that he could rebound from the off year he had suffered in 1970. The remaining players, including the newly acquired Epstein and catchers Gene Tenace and Dave Duncan, all contributed to a steady offensive attack.

As the summer progressed the Athletics showed no signs of relinquishing their lead. Blue slumped slightly, and showing his first sign of fallibility he went two weeks between his nineteenth and twentieth wins. This mini-slump cost him his chance at thirty wins. Blue won his twentieth game with a five hit shutout over the White Sox on August 7. He added to his total with another three victories in

Dress Rehearsal

August, raising his amazing record to 23-6 by the end of August. At that point Blue seemed to show increasing signs of fatigue. Having never pitched more than 172 innings in his first three professional seasons, the rigors of so many starts and so many days and nights of pitching late into those starts seemed to cost Blue as he won only one of his last seven starts, finishing his amazing season with twenty-four wins. Despite the relatively slow finish, Blue's final ERA stood at 1.82. Blue had gone the entire season after his opening day loss with an ERA under 2.00. For his efforts Blue would be rewarded with both the Cy Young and Most Valuable Player Awards for the American League.

Throughout the late summer the Athletics continued to slowly pad their lead. The team reacquired Mudcat Grant after the trading deadline but before the September 1 date on which post-season rosters are frozen. The club entered September with a seemingly insurmountable seventeen game lead over the surprising Kansas City Royals. There would be little change in those standings through the remainder of the season. When the final bell rang the Athletics had more than made up those nine games that had haunted them for the past two seasons, achieving a final total of 101 victories (the most for the franchise since the 1931 team won a remarkable 107 games) and winning the western division by a staggering sixteen games over Kansas City. Former nemesis Minnesota ended up in fifth place, twenty-six games back. It would be almost two decades before Minnesota would again be a force in the division. Catfish Hunter registered twenty-one wins to join the elite ranks of twenty game winners for the first time. Despite missing the first part of the season, Chuck Dobson contributed fifteen wins against only five losses. Jackson led the offense, bouncing back from his disappointing 1970 season with thirty-two home runs. Despite the individual accomplishments, the biggest and most important achievement for the team was clear - the Athletics were going to the post-season for the first time in forty years.

One of the many fixtures to which baseball traditionalists continued to cling as the sport entered the decade of the 1970's was the long-standing practice of playing all post-season games in daylight. Traditions like daytime-only World Series proved to be excellent fodder for the iconoclastic Charlie Finley. Finley's advocacy of nighttime post-season games, based primarily on his faith in the increased television market shares that an evening start time would bring and less altruistically by Finley's espoused concern for the inability of the common working man to watch daytime games, finally paid off when Major League Baseball agreed to pilot nighttime World Series baseball with a single night game in the 1971 World Series. It would only be fitting that Finley's Athletics should play in that game. All they needed to do to get there was beat the Baltimore Orioles in the best-of-five divisional championship series.

The Baltimore Orioles had easily captured the first two eastern division championships. Twice their opponents had been the Minnesota Twins, and twice they made short work of the Twins by sweeping them

Dress Rehearsal

in the first two League Championship Series. On paper, the Athletics of 1971 matched up rather well with the Orioles. Each team had easily won their divisions, and each had won 101 games. Position-by-position the clubs were also closely matched. The 1971 Orioles are famous in modern baseball history for having four twenty-game winners on their pitching staff. With three starting pitchers like Blue, Hunter, and Dobson, the Athletics stood a strong chance counterbalancing the Orioles twenty win club and dethroning the reigning American League Champions. Unfortunately, all was not well with the Athletics' pitching staff. Best-of-five series are very unforgiving when things do not go well, and they did not go well for the Athletics.

The trouble began in game one. As a reward for his dominance of American League hitters during the regular season, Vida Blue was given the honor of starting the first post-season game of the Charlie Finley era of the Athletics. As previously noted, the strain of a long season had taken its toll on the young left-hander, limiting him to a single victory in the entire month of September. Things started well for the Athletics as they jumped out to an early 2-0 lead on the basis of three consecutive extra base hits by Sal Bando, Angel Mangual, and Dave Duncan off Orioles' ace Dave McNally in the top of the second. The rally died when Duncan was called out after an aborted squeeze attempt by Blue. Mangual doubled home another run in the fourth, giving him extra base hits in his first two post-season plate appearances. Blue gave back a run in the bottom of the inning before working out of a difficult jam. Other than the fourth inning rally, Blue dominated the Orioles through the first six innings. Then, in the bottom of the seventh, everything came apart. Blue yielded four hits and a walk, and the Orioles scored four times to take a 5-3 lead, a lead that held through the end of the game.

Baltimore took an early 2-0 lead against Catfish Hunter in game two. The Athletics answered with a run in the top of the fourth, and the score held at 2-1 into the bottom of the seventh. Despite trailing, Williams inexplicably let Hunter bat for himself in the top of that inning as the Athletics struggled against Mike Cuellar. Another Oriole run resulting from their second home run of the day gave them a 3-1 lead in the bottom of the seventh. The gopher ball haunted Hunter again in the bottom of the eighth as Boog Powell hit his second home run of the day. Still, despite having a deep and well-rested bullpen, Williams stuck with Hunter. It made no difference; the Athletics were never able to get their offense started and they found themselves down two games to none after a 5-1 game 2 loss. One more loss and the Athletics' season would be over

With their backs to the wall, the logical Athletic starter for game three would have been fifteen game winner Chuck Dobson. But Dobson, who had begun the season on the disabled list, had fallen off badly in September by going winless after September 1. By getting knocked out of the box in the first inning against the lowly Milwaukee Brewers and delivering a poor performance against the light hitting Kansas City Royals in which he gave up three home runs, Dobson had effectively removed himself for consideration for a playoff start. In his place as the game three starter, Williams chose Diego Segui over Blue Moon Odom.

Dress Rehearsal

Segui got into trouble immediately, loading the bases before he registered his first out. He was fortunate to escape with only a single run crossing the plate in the inning. In the third inning Jackson tied the score with the very first of his incredible eighteen post-season home runs. Segui got in trouble again in the fifth, giving up two runs before giving way to Rollie Fingers. Williams emptied his bench and his bullpen, but even Reggie Jackson's second home run of the day was not enough for the Athletics to take the lead. With a 5-3 victory, the Orioles had scored their third consecutive divisional series sweep and Charlie Finley's dream of a World Series appearance was over.

1971 was a milestone year for Charlie Finley and his Athletics. Over a painful ten-year period the team had climbed from the very depths of the American League cellar to easily win their division. But a divisional championship was not Finley's goal; it was merely one step on the journey to the object of his heart's desire – a World Championship. As impressive and important as the success of the Athletics was, Finley's team had unfinished business. With the championship goal tantalizingly just out of their reach, the club would need to step up their game the following season.

The Peak

The Mustache Gang

Despite the humiliation of losing the 1971 League Championship Series, Dick Williams escaped the fate of his predecessors and was rewarded with a second season as the manager of the Oakland Athletics. With rare stability in the managerial ranks and a strong roster, Charlie Finley and his staff limited their off season trading activity. Concerns over the lack of depth in the starting pitching rotation, compounded by the questionable health of Chuck Dobson and Blue Moon Odom, drove the Athletics to focus on a search for a first-class starting pitcher to add to the club for the 1972 season. Scoring a pitcher of that caliber would not come cheaply, but the temptation of acquiring a pitcher that could put them over the top in a short post-season series drove the Athletics' willingness to sacrifice one of their key position players. On November 29 they completed a deal for Chicago Cub left-hander Ken Holtzman. The price: center fielder Rick Monday. Ironically, Holtzman was a fourth-round draft pick in the same 1965 amateur draft in which Monday had made history as the first-ever amateur draft pick. The acquisition of Holtzman was a huge leap of faith by the Athletics. The twenty-seven year-old Holtzman, once compared to the great Sandy Koufax early in his career, was similar to Catfish Hunter in that he was widely considered to be a quality pitcher who had struggled to break into the top echelon of pitchers in the early years of his career. After back-to-back seventeen win seasons in 1969 and 1970, Holtzman suffered a major setback in 1971 with a 9-15 record and a 4.48 ERA. Holtzman claimed that the only thing wrong with him was his relationship with Cub manager Leo Durocher, and that a change of scenery (and managers) was all that he needed. The Athletics believed this to be true and trusted that despite his off year, Holtzman was young, healthy, and poised for a breakthrough season. They were also frustrated with Monday's poor offensive production in 1971, to the point where the former can't-miss prospect was briefly benched in favor of rookie Angel Mangual. Confident that relatively untried youngsters Mangual, Bobby Brooks, and George Hendrick could effectively fill Monday's shoes, the Athletics decided to accept the risk and make the trade.

The team made a second attempt to deepen their starting rotation with a March deal with the Texas Rangers that brought the controversial Denny McLain to the Athletics in exchange for two rookie pitchers. While with Detroit in 1968, McLain became baseball's first thirty-game winner in three decades, a feat that has not been matched since. A twenty-four-win season followed, and McLain was rightfully considered the very best pitcher in the American League. He then self-destructed. Two suspensions in the 1970 season served as the beginning of the end of McLain's roller coaster career. McLain was sent to the Washington Senators prior to 1971. Unable to regain his prior pitching form, McLain lost an incredible twenty-two games for the Senators in 1971 while winning few friends in the locker room. As the team prepared for their transition from Washington to their new home in Texas, no tears were shed in the organization when McLain was dispatched to the Athletics.

Questions regarding the depth of the pitching staff and the strength of their centerfielders were not the only dilemmas haunting the

The Mustache Gang

Athletics as the opening of the 1972 spring training season approached. Before the spring camp could even open, a matter arose that called into question whether the 1972 season would be played at all.

The Major League Baseball Players Association (MLBPA) was formed in 1954. Faced with the heavy restrictions imposed by the reserve clause and the overwhelming power it gave club owners, the players hoped that a well-organized union would help tip the balance of power in their direction. The founding members of the Association were genuinely concerned about any potential for future work stoppages, fearing that a strike that interrupted the national pastime would put the players in a very negative light in the eyes of fans. The players nevertheless did organize, hiring labor negotiator Marvin Miller to be the MLBPA's Executive Director in 1966. Fears of a players strike were almost realized in the spring of 1969 when the opening of spring training camps was delayed by a disagreement between the union and the owners over the player pension fund. At that time players were deeply split over the concept of a strike, with many players opting to report for work over the objections and advice of their own union. But by 1972 the union had grown stronger, and a renewed battle over the pension fund and associated health care benefits set the stage for another showdown. Intense negotiations progressed throughout spring training, but when the time came to break camp and begin the season there was no agreement in place. Support for the MLBPA among the player ranks steadily grew, and by the end of March there was a strong consensus, though not unanimous agreement amongst the players, that a strike was necessary in order to satisfactorily address the pension issue. A strike was authorized for April 1, less than a week prior to opening day. Barring a miracle, the opening of the 1972 baseball season would be delayed by the sport's first organized work stoppage. Negotiations continued at a feverish pitch, but the date of the scheduled season openers came and went without a resolution of the strike. With both the owners and players losing money, there was powerful incentive for the parties to reach a compromise. Finally, on April 13, a compromise agreement was reached and April 15 was set as the opening date for the 1972 season. The first player's strike of the modern era was over for the time being, but a chain of events had been started that would change the nature of the game forever as the fundamental issues surrounding player rights continued to serve as ground zero for a series of difficult negotiations between the owners and the MLBPA.

Over a week of the playing schedule had been lost to the strike, and the practical matter of addressing the lost games had to be solved. Major League Baseball concluded that the only workable solution was to cancel every game lost to the strike, even though the number of games lost by teams varied from as few as six to as many as nine. On the basis of having lost seven games to the strike, the Oakland Athletics would play a 155 game schedule in 1972.

With the contentious collective bargaining battle between owners and players as a backdrop, the Athletics had a stalemate with one of their own players that would soon capture the national headlines.

The Mustache Gang

After his phenomenal run at the single season home run record in 1969, Reggie Jackson had sought a massive salary increase for the following season. Ever the businessman, Finley resisted and eventually won the battle by forcing Jackson to accept a salary far below what the slugger had sought. In 1972 the scene was set for another major salary confrontation between Finley and a rising superstar. This time it was 1971 pitching sensation Vida Blue that was looking for immediate entrance into the exclusive club of highly compensated Major League Baseball players. During his amazing 1971 season, Vida Blue was paid $14,750, a sum commensurate with a young prospect starting out in his professional career, but hardly the going rate for a player that had won both the Cy Young and Most Valuable Player awards or for a player that had generated so much revenue for his team by dramatically increasing the number of paying fans everywhere and every time he pitched. Blue believed he was worth more than $14,750 – a LOT more. Blue engaged an agent to assist him in his negotiation, and his initial salary demand was reported to be $115,000. Finley offered $50,000, an unprecedented raise for such a young player. Blue and his agent reduced their demand to $92,500, and it was at that point that a stalemate ensued. It was clear that player and club were so far apart that this negotiation was not going to end well. A player faced with this scenario had two options. Blue could follow the course taken previously by Jackson – he could play hardball with the owner, hold out as long as possible, then swallow his pride and cut the best deal that he could. Blue chose the second option; on March 16 twenty-two year-old Vida Blue announced that he was retiring from baseball to take a job in public relations. When the player's strike ended in April and the season finally began, the Oakland Athletics would be senselessly missing the man who was arguably the game's best pitcher.

Another improbable, off the field spring training incident would also have an impact on the 1972 Athletics, although this one would have a positive impact that indirectly drew the players together and resulted in branding the team with a new image. When the spring camps opened, Reggie Jackson reported with a full-grown mustache. Facial hair was not expressly forbidden on the Athletics or on any major league team, but part of baseball's unwritten grooming code had established the clean-shaven look as the unchallenged standard throughout the twentieth century. Jackson's mini revolution had echoed the changing norms of the times as young people across America grew their hair long and facial hair became the emblem of the young generation. Soon other Athletics followed Jackson's example. Charlie Finley was at first enraged by his loss of control resulting from this act of civil disobedience, but ever the entrepreneur he soon found a way to profit from it. Finley decreed that Father's Day would be "mustache day" in Oakland; every fan sprouting facial hair would be admitted for free on that day. Furthermore, instead of forbidding facial hair amongst his players, Finley *requested and incentivized* his field personnel to grow a mustache, offering $300 to every player that grew a mustache as part of the Father's day promotion. Even the manager and coaches were included in the promotion. Most players eagerly complied, and those that did not were eventually drawn into the program by a combination of peer pressure and not-so-subtle

The Mustache Gang

arm-twisting by Finley himself. When the big day arrived Finley made good on his $300 bonus. Many players stayed with the new look, some opting to grow beards and let their hair grow to their shoulders. Reggie Jackson's innocuous growing of a mustache in the off season had given the club one more thing to rally around. The Mustache Gang had a new nickname and a unique new look.

With few alternatives available, manager Dick Williams faced the belated season opener with what was now a patchwork starting rotation. Chuck Dobson had undergone major elbow surgery following the 1971 season and would be unavailable for all of 1972. In fact, Dobson would win only two more major league games before retiring at the age of thirty-one. Blue Moon Odom was still suffering the effects from an arm injury as well as two minor gunshot wounds received when he interceded in the burglary of a neighbor's home the previous January. Though relatively healthy after his close call, Odom was nonetheless unavailable to help much as the season opened. In desperation the Athletics signed free agent pitcher Joel Horlen, a former ace of the White Sox pitching staff who had fallen into disfavor as his performance declined and his role as a high-profile organizer within the MLBPA increased. The Athletics also signed journeyman middle infielder Tim Cullen just prior to the season opener. The latter signing would normally have been a non-event, but circumstances would later make Cullen's presence critical.

Rise and Fall

With his starting pitching ranks depleted, Williams relied solely on Ken Holtzman, Catfish Hunter, and the erratic Denny McLain as his starters for the first two weeks of the season. Hunter suffered through a slow start, but slow starts were a common flaw in the ace right-hander's career. Holtzman proved his worth immediately and pitched exceptionally well, rewarding the faith that the Athletics had placed in him when they traded Monday. McLain was a disaster. Blaming the delay caused by the player's strike for his poor performance, the former Cy Young award winner had clearly lost his velocity and no longer seemed to be a competent professional pitcher. By mid-May the Athletics convinced him to accept assignment to the minor leagues in return for allowing him to continue to receive his lucrative salary. The Athletics hoped that a few weeks in the minors would give McLain the opportunity to find his former skills, but it was not to be. McLain's performance against talent far below the major league level was no better than it had been with the Athletics. A mid-season trade saved McLain from further embarrassment in the minor leagues, but his situation did not improve upon his return to the majors with the Atlanta Braves later in the summer. 1972 would be McLain's last season in the major leagues, a tragic end to a once promising career.

As the season began it was difficult to see which, if any, of the American League western division teams could mount a serious challenge to the Athletics' goal of repeating as the divisional champions. The transplanted Texas Rangers were considered one of baseball's weakest teams. The California Angels were likewise not considered serious contenders, even with the physical and figurative arrival of the

The Mustache Gang

great Nolan Ryan. The Minnesota Twins had not completed their efforts to rebuild after their fall from glory in 1971. The upstart Kansas City Royals, second place finishers in 1971, were a strong team but were lacking the depth necessary to make a serious run for the top spot. The most improved team in the division and the early season favorite to challenge the Athletics' hope for a repeat was the Chicago White Sox. 1971 had been a rebuilding year for the Sox after several very disappointing seasons spent at the bottom of the standings. Under the guidance of second-year manager Chuck Tanner, the White Sox had added pitcher Stan Bahnsen and superstar slugger Dick (nee Richie) Allen to their roster for the 1972 season, giving them depth in both their lineup and their pitching staff unknown to them for the past several seasons.

Williams' makeshift starting rotation held together through the month of April. Odom's health improved to the point at which he was able to replace McLain in early May. While a workable solution regarding the starting pitching staff was reached, the center field situation was still in flux. A spring training injury to Angel Mangual resulted in the awarding of the starting center field job to Bobbie Brooks. After the first few weeks of the young season, Brooks was hitting well below .200 and was eventually replaced by the now healthy Mangual. Within weeks Brooks would be sent to the Detroit Tigers and his brief major league career would be all but over. But the most devastating lineup setback occurred in late April when longtime second baseman Dick Green was sidelined by back surgery. While Green was not the most productive hitter in the Athletics' lineup, he had been a force of

Rise and Fall

stability and consistency for the previous eight seasons. Worse yet, the Athletics had no apparent backup available for Green. As a stopgap measure the job was handed to veteran utility man Larry Brown, who subsequently proved to be an offensive liability. The installment of Brown signaled the beginning of a revolving door at second base, with six players cast in the role of potential replacement for Green as the season progressed.

The Athletics had personnel problems, but good teams are able to overcome such challenges and the Athletics were still a very good team. The team played very well in the first several weeks of the season and found themselves second in the standings a short distance behind the surprising Minnesota Twins.

Meanwhile, Vida Blue's days in retirement exile were about to end. Blue recognized that even at an annual salary of $50,000, every day he spent away from the club was very costly to him. For his part, Finley recognized that Blue's absence was costing the team in the standings and in revenue drawn from attendance. Still, neither side was prepared to give in. The eyes of the world seemed to be focused on the Blue holdout – even U.S. President Richard Nixon weighed in, calling Blue the "most underpaid player in sports." Finally, in an unprecedented move, Major League Baseball Commissioner Bowie Kuhn personally interceded in the stalemate. Kuhn brought the warring parties together in late April and convinced Finley to offer Blue an additional $13,000 in other benefits including a college scholarship above the $50,000 salary offer. After a few days of a tense three-way discussion, Blue agreed to the deal. The

The Mustache Gang

newly signed star reported to the team on May 2, but his long layoff left him unprepared to perform in the field for several more weeks. As a footnote to the story, Kuhn fined Finley several thousand dollars as punishment for public criticisms against the Commissioner made by Finley during the negotiation. It would not be the last time the two would spar in public, nor would it be the last time that the Commissioner would emerge with the upper hand at Finley's expense.

Vida Blue made his triumphant return to the playing field on May 24 in a relief appearance against the California Angels. He pitched only a single inning, giving up two hits, two walks, a wild pitch, and two runs. His performance was not a good omen. Blue returned to the starting rotation four days later, looking much sharper in a five inning, one hit appearance in which he struck out six opposing Chicago White Sox. Still, it wasn't until mid-June that Blue notched his first victory, a four hit shutout against the lowly Cleveland Indians. The worst fear of the Athletics and their fans had been realized – the early season layoff had severely hurt Vida Blue.

Desperate to round out the holes in their roster, the Athletics embarked on a virtually nonstop attempt to deal for talent. The most significant of these largely minor deals brought outfielder Ollie Brown to the team in mid May. Brown had begun his career with the San Francisco Giants as the latest in a line of franchise stars that included Willie Mays, Willie McCovey, and Orlando Cepeda. But Brown had not lived up to those high expectations and instead made his mark as the heart of the lineup of the expansion San Diego Padres. Brown was seen as a possible solution to the hole in center field, an experiment that ended a few weeks later with Brown being dispatched to the Milwaukee Brewers.

Meanwhile, the Athletics managed to stay embroiled in a three-way race for first place with the White Sox and the rejuvenated Twins through the month of May. The club won nine of ten games at the end of the month to take the divisional lead, a lead that they cemented with an eight game winning streak at the beginning of June. Both Holtzman and Hunter continued to pitch well, and the return of Blue Moon Odom to full strength and the unexpected contribution of rookie left hander Dave Hamilton gave the Athletics a formidable starting pitching rotation even without a significant contribution from Blue. By mid-July it appeared that the Athletics would be able to put the White Sox away and coast to their second straight divisional championship. The Athletics pounded the waiver wires after the June 15 trading deadline, acquiring Bill Voss, Art Shamsky, Orlando Cepeda, Ted Kubiak, Matty Alou, and Dal Maxvill before the post-season roster freeze date of September 1. Cepeda, acquired in exchange for the disappointing Denny McLain, was seen as an alternative to the inconsistent Mike Epstein at first base. Cepeda was hitting .298 at the time of the trade, but there were whispers that the series of knee injuries suffered earlier in his career were taking a serious toll on the slugger. The rumors proved correct – after just three pinch hitting appearances, Cepeda's season was ended due to knee surgery. The operating physician confirmed the worst – virtually all of the cartilage in Cepeda's knee was gone. Voss and Alou were targeted as potential answers to the hole in the outfield, where events had resulted in

The Mustache Gang

Reggie Jackson's transition to the center spot in an effort to field a halfway decent outfield lineup. Kubiak and Maxvill were specifically acquired to hold the fort at second base until the return of Dick Green from the disabled list. If this seemed like a lineup that was cobbled together, it was.

Alou's arrival was particularly fortuitous for the Athletics. The outfielder was a former batting champion and perennial .300 hitter, but his high salary, lack of power, and advancing age made him expendable by the St. Louis Cardinals. Displaced from the top of the Cardinal lineup by younger and seemingly more productive hitters, Alou fit the needs of the Athletics perfectly – a seasoned offensive contributor needed to fill an important gap for a few critical weeks. None of the players acquired through the waiver process were considered for long-term roles with the ballclub and it was expected that each would play their role and be dropped from the roster at the end of the season. Unlike Shamsky, Voss, and Cepeda, Alou contributed offensively to the team with a .281 batting average and 16 RBI during the stretch drive.

Green's return to duty in late August brought with it a new tactic on the part of manager Dick Williams, one that would become a trademark of the Athletics and one that would inadvertently bring with it a good deal of controversy. The removal of a weak hitting position player for a pinch hitter in the late innings was not a novel idea. Williams was undoubtedly aware that Hall of Fame manager Casey Stengel employed the technique to the extreme, once removing slick fielding third baseman Clete Boyer for a pinch hitter in the second inning of a World Series game. Beginning in late August, Williams took Stengle's approach even further. In addition to batting for the starting second baseman, Williams began to employ a rotational approach in which he would sometimes pinch hit for the second baseman every time the position came up in the batting order. With disregard for the depleting effect this had on his bench, Williams would rotate pinch hitters through the second base spot until his bench was emptied of both hitters and second basemen. In some games it was more likely that a pitcher would bat than a second baseman. In September, Dal Maxvill once started five consecutive games at second base without ever coming to bat. The bizarre tactic created the necessity to employ diverse players such as outfielder Curt Blefary and catchers Larry Haney and Gene Tenace at second base when natural infielders were no longer available.

Meanwhile, the Chicago White Sox would not admit defeat or go away. A short stumble by the Athletics in August resulted in the evaporation of their lead over the Sox. By August 12 the Athletics had lost eight out of ten games and had lost their lead as the White Sox took possession of first place on that date by beating the Athletics in eleven innings. Though the lead was literally a single percentage point, it was an infuriating setback for the defending divisional champions. Vida Blue came to the rescue the very next day, shutting out the Sox and returning the Athletics to sole possession of first place. Thus began a seesaw battle between the two teams. The White Sox took a game-and-a-half lead, but a White Sox slump and a five-game Athletics winning streak propelled

The Mustache Gang

Oakland back to the top spot in the standings. The two teams split their last four games against each other in September, robbing Chicago of an important opportunity to gain ground. The Athletics played well into the month of October, and when the dust settled and the season ended they were alone at the top of the division, five and a half games ahead of the White Sox and winners of their second straight divisional crown. In the end it was the depth of the Athletics' pitching staff, featuring twenty-one, nineteen, and fifteen win performances by Hunter, Holtzman and Odom respectively, solid relief by Rollie Fingers, strong performance by the core of the Athletics' lineup, specifically Jackson, Rudi, Bando, and Campaneris, and the contribution of newly acquired role players such as Tim Cullen, Dal Maxvill, and Matty Alou that made the difference.

The development of Fingers had perhaps the most far-reaching impact on the Athletics' season and their future success. A former American Legion Player of the Year and a 1964 *Sports Illustrated* "Face in the Crowd", Fingers had struggled to find his niche prior to the 1972 season. After rotating back and forth between the starting rotation and the bullpen in his first four major league seasons, Fingers settled in to the role of one of the era's premier relief pitchers in 1972.

And so it was that through a collection of luck, skill, and good timing that the Oakland Athletics repeated as champions of the American League western division. The team had once again given themselves a shot at making Charlie Finley's dream of winning the World Championship a reality.

The Over-the-Hill Gang

Before they could earn a trip to the 1972 fall classic, the Athletics would once again need to clear the hurdle of the League Championship Series. By this time the vaunted Baltimore Orioles had faded to a disappointing third place. With the Orioles out of the picture, the fight for the 1972 eastern division championship came down to the Boston Red Sox and the Detroit Tigers. The two teams would meet for a season-ending showdown in Detroit, a three game series beginning on October 2 with the two teams separated by a mere half game. Exciting though this was, it was also the doomsday scenario feared back in April when the players strike ended. At that time, the leagues agreed to cancel all games that were missed by the strike. It was recognized that some teams would cancel more games than others. It was hoped that this schedule disparity would have no identifiable bearing on the outcome of the pennant races. That hope was misplaced. Because of the strike, the Boston Red Sox had played one game less than the Detroit Tigers; if the pennant was decided by one game or less, one set of fans was going to be very, very upset with the scheduling arrangement. As it turned out, the home team Tigers swept the first two games of the critical series with Boston to take a game-and-a-half lead over the Red Sox and clinching the division. The Red Sox recovered to win the final game of the season, drawing to within a half game of the top and leaving resentment in the minds of Red Sox fans for decades. Whether it was fair or not, the Detroit Tigers were the 1972 American League eastern division champions.

The Over-the-Hill Gang

The Tigers had last appeared in the post-season in 1968 when they upset the St. Louis Cardinals to capture the World Championship. The core of that team was still in place in 1972. The majority of players in the Tiger lineup were over the age of thirty, including thirty-seven year-olds Norm Cash and Al Kaline. Thus, the Tigers were labeled "The Over-the-Hill Gang". And so the stage was set for the showdown between the "over-the-hill" grizzled veterans representing days gone by and the young, wild, "mustache gang", representing the new, modern era of baseball player, in a clash that would decide the championship of the American League.

Dick Williams had some basic lineup decisions to make as he faced game one of the League Championship Series. The easiest decision was to stick with Matty Alou as his right fielder, trusting that the additional offense that Alou generated would more than offset his defensive limitation and the further weakening of the defense resulting from playing Reggie Jackson in center field. While Vida Blue never did show the overwhelming dominance of American League hitters that he displayed a season earlier, he did have a decent season and was still potentially the strongest arm on the Athletics' starting staff. But Hunter, Odom, and Holtzman had been the most consistent starters throughout the season, and ace lefty reliever Darold Knowles was unavailable due to a freak late-season injury. Of the four main starters, the lefty Blue was best suited to work out of the bullpen as Knowles' replacement, and so it was that the 1971 MVP and Cy Young Award winner became the

Rise and Fall

Athletics' new left-handed stopper. Williams' toughest choices were the catcher and second base positions. Williams chose to forego Dave Duncan and his nineteen home runs, which tied him with Joe Rudi for the most by any Athletics right hand hitter, and instead rely on the relatively untested Gene Tenace behind the plate. At second base he took a gamble by relying on Dick Green. Green was cleared to play after his back surgery, but had seen limited duty in only seven September starts. Williams preferred his veteran second sacker to his other options, which included Ted Kubiak, Tim Cullen, and Dal Maxvill. With their lineup set, the Athletics appeared before the hometown crowd to face Detroit for the opening game, ready to atone for their previous playoff performance.

Game one provided a preview of the intensity and dramatic play that would highlight the five game series. Detroit took a second inning lead thanks to a solo home run by Norm Cash off of Catfish Hunter. In classic style, Hunter then proceeded to shut down Detroit for the next six innings. In the meantime, the Athletics' post-season offensive slump carried over from the previous season. In a preview of things to come, Williams sent Angel Mangual up to pinch hit for Green in the second inning, hoping to take advantage of a two-out, first-and-second opportunity to get on the scoreboard. Mangual grounded out to end the inning. In the third the Athletics tied the score on a walk, a hit, and a sacrifice fly, not exactly a staggering offensive performance. The tie held into the ninth inning, as Hunter engaged in a classic pitcher's duel with Tiger ace Mickey Lolich. The Tigers finally drove Hunter from the game with a leadoff double in their half of the ninth. At this point

The Over-the-Hill Gang

Williams brought in his newest relief pitcher, Vida Blue, to face slugger Norm Cash. Cash dropped a perfect bunt to third, and matters became worse when second baseman Ted Kubiak dropped the throw to first. With the go-ahead run on third, no outs, and right-handed slugger Willie Horton due up, Blue was lifted in favor of Rollie Fingers. Tiger Manager Billy Martin countered the move by sending left-handed pinch hitting legend Gates Brown up to bat for Horton. Fingers got Brown to pop the ball up to Bando, freezing the runners. He then ended the Tiger's hopes by forcing Jim Northrup into hitting into a double play. The Athletics were held scoreless in their half of the ninth, when Williams continued with his odd strategy choices by pinch hitting for second baseman Kubiak but letting Fingers bat for himself. Although Fingers handled a bat relatively well, it was a strange choice, particularly since he had solid relievers still available and he would need to use another player (Dal Maxvill) to replace Kubiak at second base anyway. But Williams' odd resistance to allowing second basemen to swing a bat and his confidence in Fingers drove his unusual decision. Martin countered with his own odd choice by allowing Lolich to hit for himself in the Tigers' scoreless tenth.

It started to look like Williams' confidence was misplaced when Al Kaline homered off Fingers to lead off the eleventh. Martin unwisely chose to stay with Lolich in the bottom of the eleventh. Back-to-back singles by Sal Bando and Mike Epstein proved this to be a poor decision, and Martin was forced to call on reliever Chuck Seelbach to try to douse the fire. Gene Tenace tried unsuccessfully to bunt over pinch runners Blue Moon Odom and Mike Hegan, and it appeared that the Tigers might work out of the inning. Seelbach then gave up a game-tying single to pinch hitter Gonzolo Marquez. The game-tying hit turned into a game-winning hit when right fielder Al Kaline, known for one of the greatest arms of any right fielder in history, threw the ball away when trying to catch Tenace trying to advance to third. Tenace scored easily, and the Athletics had their first post-season victory of the Oakland era.

Game two offered drama of a different and most unwelcome type. Athletic starter Blue Moon Odom shut the Tigers down, scattering three hits without walking anybody. Meanwhile, the Athletics' offense came to life. Bert Campaneris got things started by leading off the Athletics first by singling. He followed that by stealing both second and third base, taking advantage of the defensive shortcomings of Tiger catcher Duke Sims. Joe Rudi singled him home and the Athletics had all the runs they would need that afternoon. Tiger pitcher Woody Fryman held the Athletics to that single run until the fifth inning, an inning that would set off a series of events that would serve as the lasting image of this League Championship Series history. George Hendrick, pinch hitting for Dick Green, singled to start the inning. After Odom bunted Hendrick to second, Bert Campaneris came through with his third hit of the afternoon. A Matty Alou single drove home Hendrick. Reliever Chris Zachary poured fuel on the fire in his only career post-season appearance by throwing two wild pitches in the course of walking Joe Rudi. Reliever Fred Scherman then set the stage for an ugly showdown by knocking down Reggie Jackson twice before Jackson doubled to pad

The Over-the-Hill Gang

the lead to 5-0. Scherman gave way to rookie reliever Lerrin LaGrow. LaGrow began his post-season debut with an easy three-up, three-down sixth inning. In the seventh, Tiger nemesis Bert Campaneris stepped in to lead off the inning. LaGrow proceeded to hit Campaneris in the ankle with a pitch. Batters generally hate pitches thrown at their legs, and Bert Campaneris made his living with his legs. Campaneris hesitated for a split second after being struck, and then inexplicably flung the bat at LaGrow. LaGrow, his back partially turned after his follow-through, saw the approaching bat and ducked, narrowly avoiding taking a blow from the spiraling lumber. Both benches cleared as the Tigers, led by mercurial manager Billy Martin, strained to get to Campaneris. When the dust cleared Campaneris and LaGrow were both ejected from the game. Afterward, American League President Joe Cronin suspended both players for the duration of the series.

The loss of LaGrow to the Tigers was nothing compared to the loss of Campaneris. Campaneris was the fuel that drove the Athletics' offensive engine. Williams was forced to field a makeshift lineup for game three, with Matty Alou promoted to the leadoff spot and Dal Maxvill, Campaneris' replacement and a man who spent his entire career as a number eight hitter, hitting second. Perhaps not coincidentally, Tiger pitcher Joe Coleman shut out the Athletics, striking out fourteen hitters in the process.

In game four, Tiger starter Mickey Lolich began by stretching the number of scoreless innings suffered by the Athletics since the loss of Campaneris to sixteen. A solo third inning home run by Dick McAuliffe off Catfish Hunter gave the Tigers a narrow 1-0 lead which held until the seventh inning. In the top of the seventh, Mike Epstein tied the game with a solo home run. At the end of nine innings the score stood tied at 1-1. Williams was prepared to go all-out to push across the run the Athletics needed to return to the World Series for the first time in franchise history since 1931. The Athletics scored twice in the top of the tenth and the championship seemed to be within their grasp. But Williams had already used Rollie Fingers and Vida Blue to get through the first nine innings, forcing him to go to the second tier of the Athletics' bullpen. Making matters worse, Williams had compounded his tactic of endlessly pinch hitting for his second basemen by also pinch hitting for shortstop Dal Maxvill. As a result, the Athletics were out of middle infielders when they took the field in the tenth and catcher Gene Tenace was forced to fill in at second base, a move that would haunt the Athletics in the tenth. Bob Locker, Williams' choice to nail down the victory, was not sharp that day and he gave up back-to-back singles to begin the inning. Locker's replacement, Joel Horlen, was not any better, throwing a wild pitch before giving up a walk. Horlen then got Bill Freehan to hit a perfect double-play ball to Sal Bando, but substitute second baseman Tenace could not handle Bando's throw and all of the runners were safe. The Tigers now had the bases loaded with nobody out and the Athletics dream of a championship was crumbling before their eyes. With left handed hitters Norm Cash and Jim Northrup due up, Williams looked to young Dave Hamilton to save the day. Hamilton proceeded to walk Cash before giving up the game-winning hit to Northrup. If the Athletics were to win the League Championship, they

The Over-the-Hill Gang

would stop the Tigers' momentum and win the series in the Tigers' home ballpark.

Things began badly for Athletic starter Blue Moon Odom in game five. A Tiger rally in the first, assisted by a passed ball charged to catcher Gene Tenace, led to a quick 1-0 Tiger lead. The Athletics recovered in the second. Reggie Jackson, whose legendary post-season bat was largely quiet throughout this series, led off the Athletics second by walking and stealing second base, then advancing to third on a long fly out by Sal Bando. Mike Epstein was hit by a pitch before Gene Tenace struck out. With two out and runners on first and third, Williams called for a daring double steal. The Tigers read the play well, but Jackson was able to beat the throw home by inches, barreling through Tiger catcher Bill Freehan in the process. While he had failed to accomplish much with his bat, Jackson had compensated with his legs in a manner that would have made Bert Campaneris proud. Unfortunately Jackson arose from the collision with catcher Freehan grasping his hamstring. The A's top slugger had to be helped from the field; for Reggie Jackson, the 1972 season was over.

With the score tied 1-1 in the fourth, the Athletics once again resorted to "small ball" to get a much-needed run across the plate. Jackson's replacement, George Hendrick, reached on an error and was bunted to second by slugger Sal Bando. Gene Tenace singled Hendrick home, and the Athletics had a 2-1 lead. This time Williams let his starting middle infielders play as he sought to protect his narrow lead. Vida Blue came on to relieve Odom in the sixth and he made Williams

Rise and Fall

look like a genius, shutting out the Tigers on three hits over the last four innings. The Athletics were the champions of the American League.

Charlie Finley's dream of taking his team to the World Series was now a reality.

Connie Mack's Philadelphia Athletics won four American League championships from 1910-1914. The team featured (left-to-right) Stuffy McInnis, Dan Murphy, Frank Baker, Jack Barry, and Eddie Collins. McInnis, Collins, Barry, and Baker comprised Mack's legendary "$100,000 Infield".

National Baseball Hall of Fame Library, Cooperstown, N.Y.

Rise and Fall

Few baseball owners could match a record of success and controversy similar to Charles O. Finley's. Finley bought the Athletics from the estate of the late Arnold Johnson and personally transformed them from perennial cellar dwellers to World Champions.
National Baseball Hall of Fame Library, Cooperstown, N.Y.

Dick Green experienced both the difficult early years of the Finley regime and the World Championships of 1972-1974. Green possessed an extraordinary glove and a solid bat and was a steadying influence in the otherwise turbulent world of the Athletics.
National Baseball Hall of Fame Library, Cooperstown, N.Y.

The 1965 NCAA Champion Arizona State baseball team featured future Athletics Sal Bando (front row, fourth from left) and Rick Monday (back row, third from left), along with future major leaguer Duffy Dyer (middle row, fourth from left) and future A's manager Bobby Winkles (back row, far left).

Courtesy of University Archives Photographs, Arizona State University Libraries

Rise and Fall

Joe Rudi uses every inch of ballpark to snag Dennis Menke's fly ball in the ninth inning of game two of the 1972 World Series. The great Joe DiMaggio taught Rudi the finer points of playing the outfield during his short stint as a coach with the Athletics. Prize pupil Rudi became one of the finest outfielders in the game, and his famous catch became one of the lasting images of the 1972 World Series.

National Baseball Hall of Fame Library, Cooperstown, N.Y.
AP/WIDE WORLD PHOTOS

Team photo of the Oakland Athletics at the pinnacle of their success in 1973. National Baseball Hall of Fame Library, Cooperstown, N.Y.

Rise and Fall

By 1977 the Athletics had seen three future Hall-of-Famers and most of their other stars leave to reap the rewards of the newly created free agent system. In their place were a group of castaways supported by a crop of rookies, including Rob Picciolo, Mitchell Page, Mike Norris, and Wayne Gross (pictured above). Gross was an All-Star in 1977, but his twenty-two home runs were not enough to compensate for the loss of so much irreplaceable talent.
National Baseball Hall of Fame Library, Cooperstown, N.Y.

The Big Red Machine and the Great World Series of 1972

In the years following the great Yankee dynasty of the fifties and sixties, baseball had enjoyed a number of World Series performances in which upstart teams had contributed to a memorable World Series performance. Victories by the underdog 1964 St. Louis Cardinals, the 1966 Baltimore Orioles, the 1968 Detroit Tigers, the 1969 New York Mets, and the 1971 Pittsburgh Pirates had captured the imagination of baseball fans, as had the near misses by Cinderella teams like the 1965 Minnesota Twins and the 1967 Boston Red Sox. Baseball had enjoyed a series of exciting fall classics, and the 1972 World Series would be no different.

The Athletics were greeted with some good news and some bad news as they went into the series. One major concern was alleviated when baseball Commissioner Bowie Kuhn, in one of the rare decisions made by him that went in the favor of the Oakland club, decreed that disgraced shortstop Bert Campaneris would be permitted to play in the World Series. While he recognized that while Campaneris' bat throwing antics in the playoffs could not be condoned, it would be unfair to penalize the Athletics and their fans by suspending him for the World Series. Instead, Campaneris would be allowed to play in the series, but would be suspended for the first seven games of the 1973 season.

Rise and Fall

Far more disappointing was the news that Reggie Jackson's hamstring injury was serious; so serious that he would be unable to suit up for the World Series, no matter how long it went on. The Athletics were now faced with the prospect of playing the World Series without one of the premier post-season hitters in the history of the game.

The A's opponent in the 1972 World Series would be the National League Champion Cincinnati Reds. The Reds earned their moniker "The Big Red Machine" on the basis of an awesome offensive lineup. Even with a healthy Jackson in the lineup, the Athletics' lineup was no match for the Reds on a head-to-head basis. Four Red regulars, Joe Morgan, Johnny Bench, Pete Rose and Tony Perez, were recognized for their offensive abilities with election to the Hall of Fame. Of the remaining four starters, Dennis Menke was a two-time All Star, Dave Concepcion would be selected to nine All Star teams, and outfielders Bobby Tolan and Cesar Geronimo were solid players that could earn starting jobs on any team in either league. Even the Reds bench, which featured, among others, future All Stars Hal McRae and George Foster, was well stocked with offensive firepower. The Reds could hit for average, hit for power, and run the bases as well as any team in the game. Defensively, the team featured several of the top players at their positions and had no weak spots.

If the Big Red Machine had an Achilles heel, it was their starting pitching staff. Throughout their heyday of the 1970's, starting pitching would be a source of continuing frustration for Cincinnati. The Reds generally relied on a cadre of solid starting pitchers, none of who was

The Big Red Machine and the Great World Series of 1972

positioned as a dominant figure among National League starters. 1972 was no different. Where Dick Williams relied on a small core of overworked key starters, the Reds' Sparky Andersen spread his team's starts over a six-man rotation. Where Williams had three pitchers with fifteen wins or more in addition to Vida Blue, Andersen had only one – fifteen game winner Gary Nolan. Each team had strong, deep bullpens. Without Jackson, the Athletics would need to rely on their starting pitching advantage in the short series if they were to capture the World Championship against the Reds.

With Jackson unavailable for the series, Williams turned to young George Hendrick as the starting center fielder for the majority of the World Series. The twenty-two year old outfielder had exactly one hundred major league games under his belt when the 1972 post-season began. He had hit a paltry .182 with only four home runs during the regular season and had dropped to .143 in the playoffs series. In the process, Williams passed over Angel Mangual, who had a stronger regular-season performance than Hendrick. The volatile Mangual's erratic personality was matched by his inconsistent play in the field, a combination that resulted in Mangual falling out of favor with his manager. Williams moved Joe Rudi up to the number two slot in the order and Matty Alou to the number three position. Alou, a singles hitter throughout his career, had knocked in an uncharacteristically high percentage of runs in his short stint with the Athletics. Williams also chose to stick with Gene Tenace behind the plate, despite a 1-17 performance by Tenace in the League Championship Series. It was a choice that would have significant ramifications undreamed of when the series began.

Tenace repaid Williams' faith in him by slugging a two-run home run in his first World Series at bat in the top of the second. The Reds answered back with a run in their half of the inning and another in the bottom of the fourth to tie the score at two. Tenace again played the hero role, homering again in his second at bat in the fifth. Relievers Rollie Fingers and Vida Blue combined for four innings of two-hit, shutout ball and the Athletics had a 1-0 World Series lead.

Game two of the series was preceded by the last public appearance of Jackie Robinson, who spoke to the crowd prior to the beginning of the game. Robinson's appearance was arranged as part of the commemoration of his major league debut twenty-five years earlier. The diabetic Robinson would pass away from a heart attack just nine days later at the age of fifty-three.

The second game of the series was another low scoring affair. Catfish Hunter helped himself by singling home a run in the second and Joe Rudi added another run in the third with a solo home run. Hunter tamed the Reds through eight innings, scattering four hits. Hunter entered the ninth inning with a two run lead to protect. After yielding a leadoff single to Tony Perez, Hunter faced Reds third baseman Dennis Menke. Menke lined a Hunter pitch deep into left field. Left fielder Joe Rudi raced to the fence and leapt into the air after the ball. With his back

The Big Red Machine and the Great World Series of 1972

to home plate and his fully extended body almost flush against the outfield fence, Rudi pulled the liner into his glove. The catch is largely considered one of the greatest in World Series history, and the image of Rudi against that wall became one of the iconic sports images of the 1970s. But the drama was not yet over. The next batter, Cesar Geronimo, smoked a sharply hit grounder to first base. Mile Hegan, who replaced starter Mike Epstein when Epstein was removed for a pinch runner earlier in the game, made another spectacular play and retired Geronimo at first. With two outs and the runner now on second, Hunter gave up a run scoring single to pinch hitter Hal McRae. Reliever Rollie Fingers came in and got pinch hitter Julian Javier to pop out, saving the game and giving the Athletics a 2-0 edge in the Series. At that time, no team had ever won the first two World Series games on the road without going on to win the series.

Both teams would battle the elements as the series moved to Oakland. Drenching rains forced the postponement of game three and left the field a soppy mess. Game three would prove to be yet another pitcher's duel, this time between Jack Billingham and Blue Moon Odom. Game three would highlight one of the battles within the battle of this World Series. Cincinnati catcher Johnny Bench was widely considered to be in possession of the very best throwing arm of any catcher in baseball, and some credited him with having one of the best arms in history. The Athletics' lineup, minus the injured Jackson, relied heavily on the running game led by Bert Campaneris to drive their offense. This was particularly true in tight ballgames, as the first two games had been. Throughout the 1972 World Series, Bench totally shut down the

Athletics' base stealers by limiting them to a single stolen base. Campaneris himself was unsuccessful in the only steal attempt that he made. Only the veteran Matty Alou was able to successfully steal a base, while Bench nailed the three other runners brave or foolish enough to test him. In contrast, Reds manager Sparky Andersen recognized that Athletics' catcher Gene Tenace was no Johnny Bench. Inexperienced and handicapped by a much weaker arm than his famous counterpart, Tenace was totally unable to slow down the Reds base stealers. Tenace caught one out of two would-be base stealers in the first two games of the series, but the Reds were off to the races in game three, stealing successfully three times in three tries. In all, the Reds would be successful in twelve out of fifteen steal attempts before the series ended, a stark contrast to the one-for-four record of the Athletics.

The two teams were scoreless heading into the top of the seventh of game three when a Tony Perez single and a sacrifice bunt gave the Reds a runner in scoring position with one out. Cesar Geronimo followed with a single to center field, a hit that should have scored Perez easily. Center fielder George Hendrick charged the ball in a rather lackadaisical manner, all but guaranteeing that Perez would score the first run of the game. But Perez slipped and fell on the wet turf between third base and home and was a sitting duck by the time he had righted himself and continued on to home. Unfortunately for the Athletics, Bert Campaneris had taken Hendrick's belated relay throw but neglected to look toward home; he never saw Perez fall. Perez scored despite his base running gaffe, and the Reds had a 1-0 lead.

The Big Red Machine and the Great World Series of 1972

The Reds maintained their lead into the eighth, when Joe Morgan walked and the speedy Bobby Tolan singled him to third. Tolan then took advantage of Tenace and stole second. With first base open, only one out, and the dangerous Johnny Bench at the plate with a 3-2 count, Dick Williams went to the mound to discuss strategy with pitcher Rollie Fingers. Conventional wisdom called for Bench to be walked intentionally, taking the bat out of the slugger's hands and setting up a potential double play. Williams did in fact make several animated gestures to his pitcher and infielders, apparently suggesting his intention to follow the conservative path and walking Bench. Williams returned to the bench and catcher Gene Tenace stood up with his right arm outstretched in the traditional sign to complete the intentional walk of Bench. But as Fingers entered into his delivery, Tenace quickly squatted behind the plate and Fingers crossed up the Reds star with a perfect slider at the knees. Instead of walking intentionally, the shocked Bench had been called out on strikes in one of the oddest plays in World Series history, but one straight from the Dick Williams playbook. Fingers then walked Tony Perez intentionally before retiring Dennis Menke to end the rally.

Despite the A's antics, they were unable to score against Billingham and ace reliever Clay Carroll. The Reds had a 1-0 victory, and the Athletics' momentum toward the World Championship had been slowed.

Game four would be another dramatic affair. Pitchers Don Gullett and Ken Holtzman each held the opposition scoreless until Gene

Rise and Fall

Tenace hit his third home run of the series in the fifth inning. The score remained 1-0 until the top of the eighth, when the Reds answered back with two runs off Holtzman and reliever Vida Blue. Down 2-1 with one out in the bottom of the ninth, the Athletic offense finally awoke. Gonzolo Marquez started the rally with a clutch pinch-hit single. Back-to-back singles by Gene Tenace and pinch hitter Don Mincher tied the score. Pinch hitter Angel Mangual followed with a squibber through the drawn-in infield, the third pinch-hit single of the inning. The Athletics were victorious, and Williams was credited as a genius for his effective use of pinch hitters in that critical ninth inning. The Athletics were now only one game away from the championship.

A leadoff home run by Pete Rose off of Catfish Hunter did not dampen the enthusiasm of the Athletics as they attempted to close out the World Series on their home turf in game five. The club roared back as Gene Tenace smacked a three run home run in the bottom of the second, his fourth of the series (he had hit a total of just five during the *entire* 1972 regular season). Dennis Menke cut the lead to one with a solo home run in the fourth, but the Athletics answered back with another run in the bottom of the inning as a result of Gonzolo Marquez's third pinch hit single of the series. Then, with pinch runner Allen Lewis on first and Gene Tenace on third, disaster struck. Tenace was picked off third base by the rifle arm of Johnny Bench, squashing an important rally. The Reds rallied again for another run in the fifth to cut the lead to 4-3. A Joe Morgan walk and another stolen base led to the Reds tying the game in the eighth. The teams entered the ninth tied at four apiece. The Reds pushed the go-ahead run across in the ninth against Rollie Fingers and would have added to that lead had Matty Alou not thrown out Dave Concepcion as he tried to score from third on a fly ball.

With their chances for winning the World Championship in front of the hometown fans rapidly dwindling, the Athletics entered the ninth inning down by a run. Gene Tenace got things started by walking before moving to second on a well-executed sacrifice bunt by Ted Kubiak. Pitcher Blue Moon Odom then entered the game as a pinch runner for Tenace at second. This was a role that the athletic Odom filled frequently; he had stolen four bases for the Athletics during the 1972 season. Dave Duncan singled to left field, but the ball was not deep enough to allow the speedy Odom to score. With one out and runners on first and third, Bert Campaneris hit a short fly ball behind first base. Second baseman Joe Morgan sped to the point where the ball was about to land and made the catch, but stumbled after catching the ball. Odom decided that it was worth the gamble that the off-balance Morgan could not regain his posture in time to wheel around and throw him out at home. Odom was wrong. Displaying the athleticism that made him one of the premier stars of the day, Morgan did recover. Johnny Bench blocked home plate like a slab of granite, taking Morgan's throw and tagging Odom out to end the game.

The series returned to Cincinnati for game six. Disappointed by George Hendrick's poor post-season performance, Williams inserted game four hero Angel Mangual as the center fielder. Vida Blue made his first start of the series against Gary Nolan. After five games determined by a single run, game six was a blowout. Blue was knocked out of the box in the sixth inning when the Reds took a 3-1 lead. Matters got worse when the Reds roughed up Dave Hamilton and Joel Horlen for five more runs in the bottom of the seventh. In the course of the afternoon, the Reds also racked up three more stolen bases off Gene Tenace (when later asked if he thought that he would win the car that *Sport* magazine awarded to the most valuable player of the World Series, Tenace replied "even if I do the Reds will probably steal it from me"). The sloppy 8-1 loss set the scene for a dramatic seventh game showdown.

For game seven, Dick Williams chose Blue Moon Odom as his starter against the Reds Jack Billingham. Sticking with Mangual in center, Williams tried to shake up the offense by starting Dave Duncan behind the plate and moving the surprising slugger Gene Tenace to first base to replace the 0-16 Mike Epstein. The Athletics opened the scoring in their half of the first inning. Bobby Tolan misjudged a fly ball by Mangual, resulting in a three-base error. Gene Tenace further solidified his place in World Series history by driving Mangual home with a single that took a bad hop off of a seam in the Riverfront Stadium artificial turf. The score remained 1-0 until the bottom of the fifth when the Reds tied the score. The Athletics regained the lead in the sixth when Tenace drove home Bert Campaneris with his ninth RBI of the series. Sal Bando drove a pitch to center field toward fleet footed Bobby Tolan. But Tolan came up lame with a hamstring pull and Bando was safe at second with pinch runner Allan Lewis scoring on the play to make the score 3-1.

The score stood at 3-1 in the bottom of the eighth when Pete Rose led off with a single against Catfish Hunter, pitching in relief of

The Big Red Machine and the Great World Series of 1972

Odom. Dick Williams, prepared to use every single player on his team to nail down a victory, brought Ken Holtzman in to face lefty Joe Morgan. Morgan doubled, putting the tying runs into scoring position. Williams again went to his bullpen, this time calling on Rollie Fingers. Fingers retired pinch hitter Joe Hague for the first out. Williams then made a dangerous and unconventional move – he intentionally walked Johnny Bench, the potential winning run. Fingers now faced the dangerous Tony Perez with the bases loaded, one out, and the World Championship on the line. Perez hit a sacrifice fly, narrowing the lead to 3-2 and advancing the runner from second to third base. Bench stole second, putting the go ahead run into scoring position. Fingers ended the rally by retiring Dennis Menke on a fly ball. The score remained 3-2 into the bottom of the ninth. Fingers retired the first two hitters with the Reds pitcher due up. Having emptied his bench, Sparky Andersen had no option but to send Darrel Chaney, a .217 career hitter, up to pinch hit. If Fingers could retire the weak hitting Chaney, the Athletics would be the champions of the world. If not, Fingers would be facing the very dangerous top of the Reds batting order. With the pressure on, Fingers hit Chaney with a pitch. Faced with this potentially disastrous turn of events, Fingers maintained his composure and retired the great Pete Rose to end the game and the World Series.

Charlie Finley had his World Championship.

The World Takes Notice

The baseball world did not immediately grasp the significance of the Athletics first World Championship. The team was widely considered to be a very good club, featuring some of the most talented players of the era. But the long history of mediocrity established by the franchise could not be undone overnight. Other teams such as the Baltimore Orioles and the Cincinnati Reds were generally considered to be superior to the Athletics. It would still take Finley's club another year or two to truly earn a reputation as the sport's elite franchise.

What the baseball world did notice was the flamboyance and the attitude of the team, their manager, and particularly their owner. With players like Vida Blue and Reggie Jackson, outspoken, confident, spurred by their early success and subsequent high profile financial demands, the Athletics earned a very negative reputation as a cocky, abrasive group. Well publicized bickering between players only fueled the opinion that this was just not a likeable group. After all, fans surmised, why should we like them if they don't even seem to like each other? The Athletics became the team America loved to hate.

Along the way, owner Charlie Finley became the figurehead and the lightning rod for animosity against the team. United States Senator Stuart Symington once called Finley "one of the most disreputable characters ever to enter the American sport scene", an opinion shared to some degree by many. Finley's independence, his apparent indifference

The World Takes Notice

to what people thought of him and his team, and his overall attitude fueled an intense hatred of the owner that bled over to hatred of the team.

Even in the Oakland area, passion for the team, even after three World Series victories, never grew to the fever pitch that existed in other franchises. Attendance at Athletics' games was poor at best, even in the best of times.

It was under these circumstances that the development of one of history's great championship runs had begun. And in the years to follow, the characters involved in the drama known as the Oakland Athletics would only continue to feed the pool of bad feelings about the team. As the Athletics grew stronger and stronger, they became almost a caricature of themselves, the epitome of evil in the otherwise serene world of baseball. It was a persona that the team seemed to relish, but it ultimately served to diminish the world's appreciation for what an amazing collection of talent they were.

Turmoil

Charlie Finley had something to prove from the moment he purchased the Athletics. Major League Baseball owners were a stodgy, old-boys club when the upstart Finley purchased the team. Most of the clubs were family businesses, the product of old money and ultra-conservative businessmen for whom change was not tolerated, particularly when that change was promoted by a tiresome insurance man who had not yet paid his dues. Finley wanted respect, and he was not getting it from his fellow owners. Finley knew that the only way to settle the score with his adversaries was to beat them on the field – a championship team would shut their sanctimonious mouths and earn Finley the respect that he craved. And Finley knew that his players were his ticket to that championship. For that reason, Finley developed a bizarre relationship with the players in his employ. Ever conscious of his financial bottom line, Finley could be a skinflint when the mood struck him, but he could also be incredibly generous, particularly when it came to the well being of his ballplayers. By taking home the championship trophy, Finley felt he could now silence his critics and demand the respect from his fellow owners that had eluded him. That trophy also marked the beginning of a new era in Finley's relationship with his uniformed personnel. Finley wanted what everyone who wins a championship wanted – another championship. But at the same time Finley had already reached the top of his game, and from this point forward he was going to focus much more attention on finance and profit.

Turmoil

Finley saw the World Championship as a vindication of his hands-on methods, and he reacted to this success by becoming even more involved in the daily operational activities of the team, including activities occurring on the field and in the clubhouse. Dick Williams, returning for an unprecedented third season as Finley's manager, would continue to be the recipient of Finley's "advice" and direction. Williams, himself feeling that his success with the Athletics had proven that his earlier accomplishments with the Boston Red Sox were not a fluke, was not one to tolerate the increasing annoying and distracting involvement of Finley. The tension between the two men increased with each passing day.

In parallel with the widening chasm between Finley and his field personnel, the ongoing feud between the owners and the Player's Association was also in full swing as the opening of the 1973 season approached. While the source of the friction leading to the player's strike of 1972 was the somewhat esoteric topic of pension benefits, the core issue on the minds of players leading up to the 1973 season was more fundamental – the basic rights of players. Age old topics of the reserve clause, the inequitable balance of power in salary negotiations, and the unlimited ability of owners to move players between teams and between the major and minor leagues were rekindled as the Player's Association negotiated a new Basic Agreement with the owners. Mindful of the pressures of the eleventh-hour negotiations that resulted in the 1972 player's strike and the subsequent ownership concessions that were necessary to end the impasse, the owners went on the offensive in 1973. In the absence of a negotiated agreement, the owners announced that the early opening of the spring training camps, the much-awaited February arrival of pitchers and catchers in advance of the full opening of camps on March 1, would not occur unless a new agreement was in place. While technically not a lockout, this served as a clear message from the owners that they were going to play hardball with the union. Much to the relief of baseball fans, a new Basic Agreement was reached before another season disruption occurred. The new Agreement included significant changes to the nature of the owner-player relationship. Certain veteran players with the required length of service now had veto power over trades and minor league demotions. Other rules improving player compensation and limiting owner flexibility in moving players were also implemented. But the most important change was the introduction of a binding, independent salary arbitration process. Under the new program, eligible players could request the intercession of an arbitration panel during the contract negotiation process. Without this option, players were limited to two alternatives if they felt their owner's salary offer was unfair – they could grit their teeth and accept the offer or hold out and hope for a trade or a concession by the owner. Under salary arbitration, both the player and the owner would submit their last, best salary position to an independent arbitration panel. A hearing would then be held, during which each side would provide the factual basis for why their proposed salary was the appropriate one. Players and their representatives would submit the positive statistics, offer comparisons to fellow players, and emphasize their importance to their ballclub. The owners, for their part, would counter with the negative statistics and

Turmoil

recount all the ways the player had let the club down during the previous season. The decision of the arbiters was final – one of the two proposals would be selected, with no compromise. While the process would offset some of the monopoly of the power of the owners in the negotiating process, it was not without consequences; the no-compromise arbitration process clearly had a winner and a loser and often left the losing side bitter and resentful.

While the owners made many concessions in the new Basic Agreement, they did win one concession themselves. Players had an inherent advantage in the salary arbitration process resulting from the fact that they were the only party in the process that could request the intercession of the arbiters. Owners would otherwise be somewhat limited in their options for dealing with players who held out for higher salaries without requesting arbitration. The new Agreement included a clause that permitted the owners to unilaterally renew the contract of players in that situation for a period of one year. This relatively minor change would later have massive consequences.

In the aftermath of their first World Championship and with the looming specter of another labor dispute, Charlie Finley set about the task of preparing his roster for a defense of their hard won title. Vida Blue once again felt the wrath of Finley in the days leading up to the start of the 1973 season. Resentful over Blue's holdout and subsequent poor showing the previous season, Finley reportedly shopped his star pitcher,

Rise and Fall

allegedly coming to terms with the Texas Rangers on a trade that never materialized. Fortunately for the Athletics, no such trade was ever completed.

The lack of depth on the Athletics' bench and the perceived holes in the lineup were cause for concern as the Athletics entered the winter trading season prior to 1973. Great teams are traditionally "strong up the middle" – they usually have excellent players at catcher, second base, shortstop, and center field. With the exception of shortstop, those positions were the weakest in the Athletics' lineup. Dick Green retired again after the 1972 season, but once again returned at the behest of Finley. The gamble to part with Rick Monday in return for Ken Holtzman had paid off – Holtzman had been a major contributor to the club's success in 1972. But the hole in center field caused by Monday's absence was extremely problematic for the Athletics. In their very first off season trade, the Athletics sent veteran reliever Bob Locker to the Chicago Cubs for young outfielder Billy North. North was a two-time minor league base stealing champion whose early major league performance was far inferior to his strong minor league accomplishments. In addition, North was rumored to be a problem in the clubhouse. North's acquisition cleared the path for the club to ship late season savior Matty Alou to the Yankees. The Athletics then rounded out their bullpen by acquiring Horatio Pina and re-acquiring Paul Linblad, although the former acquisition forced them to surrender first baseman Mike Epstein. Epstein was never a Finley favorite and was on particularly thin ice with Finley since his emotional reaction to the Athletics' acquisition of Orland Cepeda the previous summer, when

Turmoil

Epstein saw Cepeda's arrival as a slap in the face and made his feelings public. An .094 batting average in the 1972 post-season did not help Epstein's cause. As a replacement for Epstein, the Athletics decided to move Gene Tenace to first base, leaving the catching duties to Dave Duncan. But the memories of the Cincinnati Reds running wild during the previous World Series did not sit well with Dick Williams, who wanted a stronger defensive presence behind the plate. That piece of the puzzle was filled during spring training when the Athletics sent Duncan and outfielder George Hendrick to Cleveland in return for Ray Fosse. Neither Duncan nor Hendrick were favorites of Charlie Finley. Duncan publicly criticized Finley on a number of occasions, including a brazen statement at the end of the 1970 season in which the young catcher blamed Finley for the club's second place finish. A holdout resulting from a salary dispute at the beginning of 1973 sealed Duncan's fate.

Before joining the Athletics, Fosse was famous for his appearance in the 1970 All Star game. Fosse was the catcher that Pete Rose barreled over to win the game in extra innings in one of the most well known moments of All Star history. The image of the intense Rose plowing over the young catcher to win what to some was a meaningless exhibition game, followed by the image of the triumphant Rose running from the field while Fosse rolled on the ground in agony, became one of the symbols both of Rose's career and the history of the All Star game itself. Although Fosse missed no time due to the All Star incident and he finished the season with a .307 batting average, a post-season examination revealed that the shoulder had been fractured. Fosse nevertheless came back the next season with a .276 batting average in

Rise and Fall

1971 and a second selection to the All Star team. Fosse did suffer a significant decrease in home run output and his average did drop to .241 in 1972, conditions that Fosse blamed on the collision with Rose. Despite his offensive decline, Fosse's true gift was his ability as a catcher; superstar pitcher Gaylord Perry specifically credited Fosse for his 1972 Cy Young award performance with the Indians.

As usual, the Athletics also concluded a number of other minor transactions, releasing veteran players and acquiring role players to pad their bench, including the return of prodigal son Lew Krausse and the acquisition of Billy Conigliaro, who would open the season in center field. Conigliaro, the unhappy younger brother of tragic slugger Tony Conigliaro, had announced his retirement from baseball midway through the previous season. Master salesman Finley was able to persuade Conigliaro to return to uniform with the Athletics.

Despite the acquisition of North and Fosse, the Athletics still had one new, huge gap to fill, one that they had not anticipated at the conclusion of the previous season. For years, partially at the urging of the iconoclastic Charlie Finley himself, Major League Baseball had debated the idea of introducing a new role to the game – the role of a hitter who would bat in place of the pitcher and never play the field. The purpose of this "designated pinch hitter" was twofold – to further contribute to the generation of additional offense, a major goal of the owners since the pitching-dominated late 1960's, and to extend the careers of aging stars, stars who were unable to effectively play positions in the field but were still able to swing a powerful bat. As with any

Turmoil

radical change, this proposal had many detractors, particularly among National League owners. But Finley was able to convince his fellow American League owners to try the rule for 1973, and the new designated hitter position was born. Ironically, the designated hitter favored teams with deep benches or a stockpile of aging sluggers, neither of which applied to the Athletics. Orlando Cepeda, crippled by multiple knee surgeries but still able to swing the bat effectively, was a model for the new designated hitter rule, but the Athletics had given up on him after his most recent knee surgery and released him the previous December. Cepeda signed with the Boston Red Sox, becoming one of the most effective early designated hitters. Another former Athletic, Tommy Davis, was likewise considered to be a classic designated hitter; unfortunately, Davis was now in the employ of the Baltimore Orioles. Pinch hitting sensation Gonzalo Marquez seemed like a natural fit for the position; Marquez had already established a keen ability to hit from the bench and had never hit below .282, once hitting .341 at the AAA level. But Marquez was not highly regarded by the Athletics, perhaps owing to his season-long holdout in 1971. Marquez was also neither a fast base runner nor a power hitter, two traits that Finley considered prerequisites for the designated hitter role. Unable to find a suitable candidate to fill this new role, the Athletics were forced to open the season with Billy Conigliaro in center field and a patchwork array of designated hitters led by Billy North. North was a total contrast to most of the other designated hitters in the league – he was a young, speedy, singles hitter while most of his counterparts were veteran sluggers, many of whom could barely run the bases.

Rise and Fall

The 1973 season began poorly for the revamped Athletics, as they lost six of their first eight games and closed out April in fifth place. In an effort to stimulate the Athletics' offense, two major lineup changes were attempted. As a solution for their designated hitter woes, the Athletics acquired veteran slugger Deron Johnson from the Philadelphia Phillies. Johnson had played briefly for the Athletics during the very beginning of the Charlie Finley era before being shipped to the Cincinnati Reds. Johnson enjoyed several very productive seasons in the National League, winning the league's RBI championship in 1965. But throughout his career Johnson was considered a liability in the field – a man without a position who was moved between third, first, and the outfield depending upon the needs of the team at the time and his manager's estimate of where he could do the least defensive damage. Out of such material many of the original designated hitters were born. Johnson's availability was made possible by concerns that his once formidable bat was weakening; the Athletics hoped that the role of designated hitter would rejuvenate the aging slugger. Their gamble paid off – Johnson was the second most productive designated hitter during the inaugural season for that role. The only designated hitter with greater offense output was Boston's Orlando Cepeda, the same Orlando Cepeda written off by the Athletics prior to the season.

If the addition of Johnson was a typical early season adjustment of the nature taken by many teams in order to round out their lineup after a few weeks of regular-season action, the second lineup change was anything but routine. During the 1972 season, Dick Williams had established a habit of rotating players through the second base position during the course of a game. It was not unusual for Williams to lift the starting second baseman for a pinch hitter in the early innings, then continuously pinch hit for the replacements as the game progressed. This practice carried over into the 1973 season, with starting second baseman Dick Green's plate appearances often limited to one or two a game. In his first eighteen starts of the season, Green was limited to thirty-seven at bats. Green did not help his cause by starting the season with an 0-12 slump, and by May 4 he was hitting only .189. It was then that Williams decided to limit his perceived offensive liability at second base even more. He had the option of benching Green in favor of Dal Maxvill or Ted Kubiak, the latter of who was hitting .286 at the time. Instead, Williams elected to take the designated hitter concept a step further; he would take extreme measures to minimize plate appearances by his second base crew. For the May 4 game in Cleveland the number two hitter in the lineup was left hand hitting, left hand throwing "second baseman" Gonzolo Marquez, who was hitting .357 at the time as a pinch hitter and designated hitter. Marquez had never played second base and he was never intended to actually play the field at that position. Williams' plan was to use Marquez in the top of the first, replace him with Green or some other real second baseman when the team took the field in the bottom of the inning, then pinch hit for Green and his successors as situations dictated and as long as he had suitable players on the bench. Over a six game period, Jay Johnstone, Billy Conigliaro, and Angel Mangual all took turns in that role. During that period, the starting pseudo second basemen went a combined 0-5 with a walk. The bizarre experiment ended on May 10 with Green back in the starting role as a contributor to a 17-2 blowout of the Texas Rangers, a game which

Rise and Fall

saw Green batting a season-high six times. For the remainder of the season Green would continue to be the regular, starting second baseman, although he would still be frequently lifted for a pinch hitter.

The end of the "extreme rotation" at second base coincided with the Athletics' climb above the .500 mark. The White Sox had begun the season at a sizzling pace and again looked like the team most likely to give the Athletics a run for their money. But with a starting pitching staff that still featured Catfish Hunter, Ken Holtzman, and a reinvigorated Vida Blue, nobody believed that the Athletics would wallow at the .500 mark for long. Yet as the month of June arrived, that was right where the Athletics found themselves. Making matters worse, it appeared that the balance of power in the league was shifting westward; as late as June 9 the Athletics were still stuck in fifth place, despite a .500 record. By the end of June the Athletics had slowly climbed to first place, but only one and a half games separated the top five teams in the division. Only the lowly Texas Rangers had dropped from contention.

On the mound, Vida Blue was still struggling to regard his 1971 form, but Hunter and Ken Holtzman were among the league's winningest pitchers. Reggie Jackson and Sal Bando were enjoying outstanding seasons, Deron Johnson provided much needed pop from the designated hitter position, and Johnson's arrival had freed Billy North to play center field on a daily basis. North repaid the Athletics' faith in him by surpassing Bert Campaneris as the team's top base stealer, further helping to drive the Athletics' recovering offense. The combination of

Turmoil

the veteran Campaneris and the young North gave the Athletics the very best base running duo in the league.

As with previous seasons, the 1973 Athletics made frequent use of the waiver wires to add needed depth to their bench. After the trading deadline, the club acquired Jesus Alou, who followed in the footsteps of brothers Felipe and Matty to become the third Alou brother to play for Finley's club. The team also acquired infielder Mike Andrews, pinch hitting legend Vic Davalillo, and Rico Carty. In addition, the team completed an unusual trade in which they sent 1972 World Series hero Gonzolo Marquez to the Chicago Cubs in exchange for Pat Bourque. Of all the newcomers, it was Alou that had the greatest impact down the stretch. For the second season in a row, an Alou brother plugged an important hole in the Athletics' outfield as Jesus filled in for the injured Joe Rudi in August, hitting a robust .306.

The Athletics played steady baseball through the month of July, opening a slight lead that was later closed by the Kansas City Royals. At the end of the month the Athletics found themselves tied for first with the Royals. It was about that time that things began to come together for Vida Blue, who went 11-2 over the last two months of the season. The Royals knocked the Athletics from the top spot briefly in early August, opening up a two game lead over the Athletics on August 10. The Athletics rebounded to win thirteen out of fourteen against eastern division opponents, including a nine game winning streak. By this time the White Sox, Twins, and Angels had all fallen off badly, leaving the Royals as the only team with any hope of catching the red hot Athletics.

Rise and Fall

The Royals closed the gap by beating the Athletics two out of three times in an early September series, but a six game winning streak in mid-September gave the Athletics the cushion they needed to cruise to their third consecutive divisional championship. Even with the club losing six of eight in the final weeks of the season, the Athletics were safely ahead of the Royals. The final standings had them six games ahead of the Royals, but the relatively flat finish by the club was a cause for concern as they headed into the post-season.

The Athletics' opponents for 1973 American League Championship would be the Baltimore Orioles in a rematch of the ill-fated 1971 playoff series. As they had after their setbacks following their 1966 World Championship, the Orioles had undergone a minor retooling program to ramp up their attack after finishing third in 1972. Gone were Frank Robinson, Don Buford, and Dave Johnson; in their place were a new wave of stars such as Bobby Grich, Don Baylor, and Earl Williams. Their designated hitter was Athletics castoff Tommy Davis, regarded by some as the best designated hitter in the game. The pitching staff was still formidable, featuring the remarkable trio of Dave McNally, Jim Palmer, and Mike Cuellar. And the Orioles were healthy, with their full contingent ready and able to take on the western division champs. The Orioles were a significant obstacle on the path to a second World Championship, and the memory of the 1971 League Championship Series sweep at the hands of Baltimore was seared in collective consciousness of the Athletics.

Turmoil

Injuries again played a role as the Athletics prepared for the 1973 post-season. Billy North missed the last two weeks of the season with an injury and entered the post-season with a questionable status. As they had in the 1972 World Series, the Athletics would be forced to perform without one of their key outfielders and a key component of their offensive attack. But the Athletics were a great team, and great teams overcome such obstacles. And this time the Athletics were prepared. This time they were a seasoned team, tested in the heat of post-season competition.

With Angel Mangual in the lineup in the place of the injured North, the 1973 American League Championship series began on an ominous note for the defending champions as Vida Blue continued his history of post-season struggles. He failed to get out of the first inning of game one, yielding three hits and two walks, putting the Athletics in a 4-0 hole from which they never emerged. In the meantime, Oriole ace Jim Palmer made short work of the Athletics, shutting them out 6-0. Along the way Palmer scattered five hits, two by Vic Davalillo, who pinch hit for Ray Fosse and stayed in the game at first base. If the Athletics' offense did not come to life quickly, the series would be lost as it had been two years earlier.

To the great relief of the Athletics, the offense did just that in game two. Bert Campaneris sent the Orioles an early signal of what kind of day it would be by greeting starter Dave McNally with a leadoff home run in the top of the first. The Orioles answered back with a run of their own against Catfish Hunter in the bottom of the inning. The score remained deadlocked as the two All Star pitchers traded goose eggs into the top of the sixth, when Joe Rudi and Sal Bando started the inning with back-to-back home runs. Once again the Orioles shot back with another run in the bottom of the inning, closing the score to 3-2. But the Athletics' power machine was not done yet, as Bando hit his second home run of the day, a two run shot in the eighth that sealed an eventual 6-3 victory that evened the series at 1-1 in time for the Athletics' return to Oakland. It was the first time that the Orioles lost a League Championship Series game, having swept three series and starting the current series with their game one victory. For Bando, it was the finest post-season performance of his career; in addition to his two home runs and three RBI, he was robbed of a third home run by a spectacular second inning catch by Al Bumbry. Things were now starting to look brighter for the Athletics.

Game three featured a classic pitcher's duel between star pitchers Mike Cuellar and Ken Holtzman, a contest of the nature that may never be seen again. Holtzman yielded a solo home run in the second inning, but the Athletics scratched out the tying run in their half of the eighth, thanks partly to a well-executed sacrifice bunt by pinch hitter Mike Andrews and good base running by pinch running specialist Allen Lewis. Both starters remained in the game into the eleventh inning, each limiting the opposition to a mere three hits. The game ended when Bert Campaneris, leading off the bottom of the eleventh, hit his second home run of the series to win the game. For Campaneris, the two home runs equated to half of his total regular-season output of four.

Turmoil

With a chance to finish the Orioles off in game four, the Athletics sent Vida Blue to the mound to redeem himself for his game one disaster. The Athletics got off to the start they needed, knocking ace Jim Palmer from the game with a three run second inning rally. With Blue pitching a two-hitter and protecting a 4-0 lead in the top of the seventh, the Athletics were nine outs from repeating as League Champions. It was exactly the scenario Dick Williams had hoped for; a late inning lead and a well-rested bullpen at the ready. Then it all fell apart. Blue stumbled, and an unexpected home run from weak hitting Oriole catcher Andy Etchebarren had tied the score at 4-4 by the time reliever Rollie Fingers entered the game. A Bobby Grich leadoff home run off Fingers in the eighth gave the Orioles a 5-4 lead, a lead that the Athletics could not overcome. The series would hinge on a deciding fifth game.

The Athletics prepared for their fateful showdown in their own unique style – they fought. This time the combatants were Blue Moon Odom and Rollie Fingers, who engaged in a clubhouse brawl that started over comments made by Fingers that Odom interpreted as a knock on his friend Vida Blue. The two had been needling each other for most of the season, and on this day the situation erupted into an all-out fight. Fingers took the worst of it, ending up with a number of stitches courtesy of cutting his head on a locker. On the positive side, battle may have served to release some of the tensions that were building among the Athletics' players.

Rise and Fall

Catfish Hunter's Hall of Fame plaque includes the words "The bigger the game, the better he pitched". Game five was a very big game indeed. As was his habit, Catfish Hunter rose to the occasion. While Hunter stymied the Orioles bats, the Athletics scored three early runs to chase surprise Oriole starter Doyle Alexander from the game. Oriole manager Earl Weaver opted to bring Jim Palmer, fresh off of his disappointing game four performance, in from the bullpen to stop the bleeding, and stop it he did. But the damage was done, and Hunter kept the door closed on the Oriole offense. Scattering five hits over nine innings of work, Hunter delivered a 3-0 shutout for his second playoff victory. The Athletics had their revenge on the Orioles and were once again the champions of the American League

Battling the Upstarts - The Second Great World Series

At the conclusion of the 1973 regular season, most of the baseball world expected and perhaps relished what appeared to be a certain rematch of the 1972 World Series between the Oakland Athletics and the Cincinnati Reds. While the Athletics held up their end of the bargain, the Reds had not counted on running into a phenomenon in the form of the New York Mets.

When the major leagues were split into two divisions, one of the primary objections that baseball purists had raised was that a relatively weak team that finished first in a poorly performing division could get hot in a short five game playoff series and conceivably upset a far superior team. If such an upset would occur, the regular season would be rendered unimportant and the best team would not represent their league in the ensuing World Series. There were no such upsets in the first four seasons of divisional play. Of the eight playoff series played during those first seasons, the 1972 Cincinnati Reds were the only team with the lowest winning percentage to win their League Championship Series, and in their case they were only two percentage points below their opponents. But 1973 would be different. To begin with, the Athletics won three fewer games than the opposing Baltimore Orioles. In the senior circuit, the story was even more extreme. In the National League, four western division teams won at least as many games as the eastern division champion Mets. The Mets emerged triumphant after a season long struggle that had all six divisional teams in contention. As most of the teams knocked each other off during the month of September, the

Rise and Fall

Mets got red hot and won nine of their last eleven games to rise from four games under .500 in fourth place, three and a half games out of first, to the divisional championship. Their final winning percentage of .509 made them the poorest performing first place team in major league history. They entered their playoff with Cincinnati on a high note but as heavy underdogs. Still, the Mets proved their strong finish was no fluke, and as they had four seasons earlier they used a rock solid pitching staff to triumph over a heavy hitting opponent in the League Championship Series. When it was all over, the Mets had beaten the stunned Reds in a wild five game series.

Even a victory over the Big Red Machine could not earn respect for the Mets as the 1973 series began. The swaggering Athletics cut a menacing figure for the underdog Mets, and it seemed that everyone other than the Mets and their loyal fans expected the Athletics to make short work of the pretenders from New York.

Not unexpectedly, the series opened with controversy. The Mets refused to allow Finley and the Athletics to add second baseman Manny Trillo to the Athletics' World Series roster. When the Athletics submitted their post-season roster to the Commissioner's office at the August 31 deadline it included rookie catcher Jose Morales. The Athletics then foolishly chose to sell Morales to the Montreal Expos on September 18, putting them in the position of facing the post-season one player short. The Athletics formally requested permission from the Mets to use Trillo as a replacement for the roster spot previously filled by Morales. The Mets refused to grant permission, which was well within

Battling the Upstarts - The Second Great World Series

their rights. With the injured Billy North likely unavailable for the Series, the Athletics were faced with the prospect of taking on the Mets with only twenty-three players, two short of the permitted amount. Veterans Jesus Alou and Vic Davalillo would replace North in the lineup as the Athletics prepared to defend their title with the knowledge that the last team other than the New York Yankees to win back-to-back World Series was none other than Connie Mack's Philadelphia Athletics way back in 1929-1930.

Game one offered a foretaste of how tight the series would be. Starter Ken Holtzman was hit hard, but managed to hold the Mets scoreless through the first three innings. A double by Holtzman, an error by the normally sure handed Felix Millan and some excellent base running by Bert Campaneris gave the Athletics a 2-0 lead in the third inning, spoiling an otherwise fine pitching performance by Jon Matlack and giving the Athletics a lead that was never relinquished. Dick Williams called on Rollie Fingers to safeguard a 2-1 lead in the sixth inning, and Fingers delivered three and a third scoreless innings of relief. Darold Knowles relieved Fingers in the ninth to nail down the victory. Millan's error would not be the last time that an error by a second baseman would impact the outcome of the game, but at the time it passed with little controversy, with the recognition that errors were an inevitable part of the game.

As it had in 1972, game two delivered some of the greatest drama of the series. In what would be a seesaw affair, the Athletics greeted Met starter Jerry Koosman with three extra base hits and two runs in the bottom of the first. Cleon Jones answered back with a solo home run off Vida Blue in the second, but the Athletics scored again in the bottom of the inning. Wayne Garrett hit the Mets second home run in the third to cut the lead to 3-2. The Mets kept the lead at one by picking Gene Tenace off from third base in the bottom of the third, killing the Athletics' third rally of the day. The Mets erupted for four runs in the sixth, knocking Blue from the mound and giving the Mets a 6-3 lead. Mets manager Yogi Berra called on ace reliever Tug McGraw to hold back the Athletics in the bottom of the sixth. The Athletics managed to scratch out another run in the seventh, cutting the Mets lead to 6-4. In a seemingly innocuous move, Dick Williams sent Mike Andrews up to bat for Ted Kubiak in the bottom of the eighth. After grounding out to end the inning, Andrews took over Kubiak's spot at second base.

After a leadoff single by Rusty Staub in the ninth, Berra called on Willie Mays as a pinch runner. It was a logical move – Mays, even at forty-two, was a more effective base runner than Staub, and Mays would also be an upgrade over the injured Staub in the outfield. But in an embarrassing turn of events, Mays missed second base when John Milner singled to right, returning to the bag safely but possibly costing the Mets a much-needed insurance run.

McGraw took the mound in the bottom of the ninth, prepared for his fifth inning of relief work. A workhorse who averaged almost three innings per appearance during the regular season, McGraw had already pitched two innings the previous day. Nonetheless, Berra calculated that

Battling the Upstarts - The Second Great World Series

a tired McGraw was a better hope than his more rested alternatives. Pinch hitter Deron Johnson, relegated to the bench since the designated hitter rule was not in effect during the series, led off the bottom of the ninth with a line drive to center field. Mays, whose regular season and World Series outfield play was legendary, misplayed the ball and it fell for a double. This opened the door for a two out Athletics' game-tying rally. The game would go into extra innings.

The Mets had another opportunity to put the game away in their half of the tenth inning. A single, a sacrifice, and a Gene Tenace error put Bud Harrelson on third base with one out. Felix Millan lifted a short fly ball to left field and Harrelson decided to challenge Joe Rudi's arm by tagging up and heading for home after the catch. Catcher Ray Fosse blocked Harrelson's approach to home plate, forcing the lightweight Harrelson to choose between trying to go through or around Fosse. He chose to go around him. Fosse made the catch and swiped at Harrelson. In the first controversial play of the series, Harrelson was called out. Video replays seemed to show that Fosse missed the tag, but the umpire's call stood. A fraction of an inch changed the outcome of the game and of the World Series.

Ace relievers Fingers and McGraw held their opponents as the game entered the top of the twelfth. Fingers was on the verge of working out of a Met rally, getting two difficult outs after the Mets had placed runners on first and third. Back-to-back singles gave the Mets a two run lead and chased Fingers from the mound. It was then that matters took an ugly turn for the Athletics, resulting in one of the darkest chapters of the team's history. John Milner hit what should have been an inning ending ground ball to second baseman Mike Andrews, but the ball skipped through the normally slick fielding infielder's legs. Andrews' day got even worse when the next play also came his way; this time an awkward throw pulled Tenace from the bag and resulted in another Met run and a second error for Andrews. Berra stuck with McGraw in the bottom of the inning, stretching his ace for an amazing seventh inning of relief. The obviously tired McGraw yielded a triple by Reggie Jackson and a walk to Tenace before being mercifully relieved by George Stone. Stone worked out of the jam with only a single run scoring; it was not enough for the Athletics and the Mets had tied the series with a 10-7 victory.

It would be an understatement of the highest order to say that Charlie Finley was disappointed that his team had failed to finish off the Mets in game two, and Finley was not a man to take disappointment lightly. In this case, Finley chose the unfortunate Mike Andrews as his scapegoat. When Finley acquired Andrews from the White Sox in order to provide some depth for his second base rotation, it was well known that Andrews was suffering from a chronically sore throwing shoulder. Prior to his release by the White Sox, Andrews had been used primarily as a first baseman for the first time in his career. Upon signing Andrews, Finley told him that he would be used exclusively as a pinch hitter and occasional designated hitter. Nevertheless, situations like the extra inning game and the use of second basemen Dick Green and Ted Kubiak earlier in game two put Andrews in the field for several innings. Finley resolved to take steps to ensure that it would be the last time that

Battling the Upstarts - The Second Great World Series

Andrews appeared in the field. Not wanting to restrict his team's ability to maneuver, Finley devised a plot to get second basemen Manny Trillo added to the roster. After game two ended, Finley called Andrews into a meeting with Athletics' team doctor Harry Walker. Finley presented Andrews with a written statement, asserting that Andrews was suffering from an injured shoulder that rendered him incapable of playing any more in the World Series. Andrews refused to sign a document that he knew to be completely false. Andrews later acknowledged that Finley never overtly threatened him in any way, but Finley did apply significant psychological pressure to Andrews throughout that night. Andrews, later claiming that Finley "wore him down", eventually signed the attestation. Finley then forwarded the statement to Commissioner Bowie Kuhn with a formal request to add Trillo to the roster to replace the "disabled" Andrews. Finley's ploy had three immediate results. First, it generated uproar among the Athletics' players. As they had after Finley's 1967 suspension of Lew Krausse, the players contemplated striking unless Andrews was permitted to remain on the active roster. Part of the players' motivation was loyalty to the likeable Andrews, part was driven by their growing hatred of Finley, and part was a result of their recognition that any one of them could find themselves the target of Finley's wrath and similar tactics in the future. While the players eventually conceded that the World Series was too important an obligation to sacrifice for Andrews, several players did create a makeshift protest by taping Andrews' number seventeen to their uniform sleeves. The second impact was on manager Dick Williams. Williams had tired of Finley's meddling long before that fateful day, and the Andrews incident was the last straw. Williams decided on that day that

Rise and Fall

three seasons as Charlie Finley's manager was enough – he would walk away from his job after the World Series, regardless of the outcome. Finally, Commissioner Kuhn reacted swiftly and certainly. Andrews, he declared, was to be immediately reinstated and Trillo would not be permitted to join the Athletics' roster. In addition to his clear recognition of Finley's Machiavellian nature, Kuhn stated in a memo to Finley and the Mets that there was "No suggestion that his (Andrews) condition had changed or worsened since the series began or that he was injured during the series", noting the fact that Andrews was healthy enough to play in game two. In the meantime, Andrews had returned to his home in Massachusetts, leaving the Athletics another player short going into game three.

When the series moved to New York for the third game, the hometown Mets fans were at a fever pitch. Their club's unexpected rise to the top of the division, the upset over the Reds, and the Andrews controversy all served to ignite the already volatile fans. Finley was firmly cast in the role of Antichrist and Finley had created a martyr in the form of Mike Andrews. While the Athletics would be three players short for game three, the Mets crowd would serve as an effective twenty-sixth man for their team.

Game three featured a pitcher's duel between future Hall of Famers Tom Seaver and Catfish Hunter. The Mets jumped on Hunter to take a quick 2-0 lead in the first, but the Athletics chipped away and eventually tied the score in the eighth inning. When regulation play ended, the two teams were still tied. For the second time there would be

Battling the Upstarts - The Second Great World Series

extra innings. Berra again relied on the rubber-armed Tug McGraw, but the weary McGraw could only deliver two innings. The Athletics touched his replacement, Harry Parker, for an eleventh inning run and Rollie Fingers held the Mets scoreless for the save, giving the Athletics a 2-1 series lead.

Mike Andrews was active, in uniform, and on the bench for the fourth game of the series. Williams went out of his way to pose for press photos along side of the disgraced player, setting the stage for one of the most bizarre events in World Series history. The game was over early, with the Mets knocking starter Ken Holtzman out in the first inning with a three run rally. The score stood at 6-1 in the top of the eighth when Dick Williams stole the moment with the ultimate act of defiance against Finley. In need of a right-handed pinch hitter, Williams seized the chance to send Andrews to the plate. Met fans responded with a unanimous standing ovation when Andrews was announced. It is safe to say that the Shea Stadium crowd had likely never showered such a reception on a .200 hitter, let alone one that played for an opposing team in a World Series game. The vast majority of them had probably never heard of Mike Andrews a week prior. Such was the level of hatred New Yorkers felt for Finley. Andrews grounded out, prompting another huge ovation as he left the field.

It would be Mike Andrews' last appearance in a major league game.

Rise and Fall

The Athletics put themselves in a very difficult situation by losing game five by a score of 2-0. The Athletics' bats went dormant against Met starter Jerry Koosman, who combined with the ubiquitous Tug McGraw to hold the Athletics to three hits. The Athletics now found themselves with their backs to the wall, down 3-2 in the series. If the Athletics were going to repeat, they would need to win both of the final two home games.

Dick Williams endeavored to wake up the Athletics' offense by benching the slumping Ray Fosse in favor of Deron Johnson, placing Johnson at first and moving Tenace behind the plate. While Johnson did not contribute materially to the Athletics' offense, the bats did awaken, with Reggie Jackson leading the way. Jackson hit two doubles, driving in two runs and scoring a third. The rematch between Seaver and Hunter resulted in a 3-1 Athletic victory.

For the second year in a row, the Athletics would be playing a seven game World Series.

Not since the dead ball era had a team gone through a seven game World Series without hitting a home run. The 1973 Oakland Athletics, third in the American League with 147 regular-season home runs, were faced with joining that inglorious group by going homerless in the first six games. One of the top offenses in the game had suffered a loss of energy in their powerhouse. The drought ended in the bottom of the third when home runs by Bert Campaneris and Reggie Jackson gave

Battling the Upstarts - The Second Great World Series

Ken Holtzman a 4-0 lead. An insurance run in the fifth gave the team a safe 5-0 lead. A ninth inning Met rally was insufficient to cut the lead and the Athletics clinched the World Series with a 5-2 victory. The Athletics had joined the elite teams in history by repeating as World Champions.

Less than two weeks after the Athletics' historic victory, Mike Andrews was given his unconditional release. Having been released twice in 1973, and with the stigma of a sore shoulder and his role in the World Series controversy hanging over his head, Andrews' prospects for finding work with another major league team were virtually nil. While his former teammates were home celebrating their victory and looking forward to a potential third championship in 1974, twenty-nine year-old Mike Andrews was facing the end of his major league career. Other than a short stint in Japan, Andrews' career as a professional baseball player was over. Andrews sued Finley, a suit that was eventually resolved with an undisclosed settlement in 1978.

1973 was a milestone season for Reggie Jackson. Jackson caught the attention of major league scouts during his short but productive time at Arizona State and shot to national prominence with his historic chase of the home run record in 1969. Sporting a .258 career batting average going into 1973, Jackson had established himself as a very solid if inconsistent power hitter, but RBI totals of 66, 80, and 75 in the years leading up to 1973 indicate that he was still not a dominant offensive force. All of that changed in 1973. Jackson worked hard to earn recognition that would match his massive ego, and he delivered the finest overall offensive performance of his career to that point. Posting a .293 batting average, Jackson blasted a league high 32 home runs while knocking in 117 runs, also the best in the league. When it came time to select the 1973 American League Most Valuable Player, all twenty-four voters selected Reggie Jackson as their choice. With two World Championships, a home run title, and a unanimous MVP award on his resume, Reggie Jackson had clearly joined the game's elite. Still bitter from years of nasty salary negotiations, often marked by public criticism of the outfielder by the A's owner, Jackson was locked and loaded for his next round of salary talks. It was payback time, and Reggie was determined to make Charlie Finley compensate him at a level befitting the very best player in the league.

Hardball

Charlie Finley was now the owner of an acknowledged powerhouse. His team's back-to-back World Championships had earned them a well-deserved spot at the very top of the sport. But such success does not come without cost. Finley's stars were now considered among the game's elite, and they wanted to be compensated at their full value. Finley's inability to transform his success on the field into comparable financial success, coupled with his intense focus on expenses and the bottom line, limited the amount that he would willingly spend to pay his ballplayers. The man who once set sky-high targets on how much he was willing to invest to build his team was now setting a very low ceiling on how much he was willing to reward those same players for their performance.

It was therefore no surprise that Reggie Jackson and Charlie Finley could not agree on the amount of Jackson's salary for 1974. The owner begrudgingly offered Jackson a $25,000 raise to make him a member of the elite $100,000 salary club. Jackson rejected the offer, holding out for a $60,000 raise to $135,000. In any other year, the stage would have been set for a showdown that would have likely resulted in a Jackson holdout, jeopardizing his availability for the start of the 1974 season. But a new era of player / owner negotiations had begun. For the first time, the option of salary arbitration was available in the spring of 1974. Predictably, Charlie Finley's Athletics had more cases before the arbitration board than any other team.

Rise and Fall

Nine Athletics, including 1973 American League Most Valuable Player Reggie Jackson, sought redress through the salary arbitration process. Jackson, Sal Bando, Ken Holtzman, Rollie Fingers, and Darold Knowles all won their arbitration cases. Jackson and Bando were the big winners; Jackson received his $60,000 raise to an annual salary of $135,000, and Bando also joined the elite six-figure salary community with a $40,000 raise that brought him to an even $100K salary. Joe Rudi, Gene Tenace, Ted Kubiak, and reserve infielder Jack Heideman all lost their cases. Rudi received a paltry $5,000 raise to $55,000. Tenace's salary settlement was $45,000 – just a few thousand dollars greater than utility man Kubiak's salary, a fact that rankled the slugger as the new season began.

Regardless of which side won the arbitration battles, one thing was consistent – the loser carried the bitterness of the loss forward through the coming seasons. The residual impact of the first salary arbitrations on the relationship between Finley and his star players would have serious consequences in the future.

Help Wanted

Not even Charlie Finley would willingly change managers after winning back-to-back World Championships. But this time the owner of the Athletics would not be the one to decide whether his manager stayed or went.

Rumblings of discontent began coming from manager Dick Williams during the 1973 season. A variety of factors were likely playing on Williams' mind. Finley was a constant irritant, constantly interfering with Williams' management of the team on the field. And Williams, on course for what was to be his fourth first-place finish in his first six years as a major league manager after winning two championships in his two years of managing at the minor league level, almost certainly recognized that he was now a valuable commodity and likely to make a significantly higher salary should he end up in the open market. For his part, Williams began making noise about wanting to work on the east coast, closer to his home in Riviera Beach, Florida. This was undoubtedly a smokescreen for his real motives, as evidenced by the fact that Williams' future stops as a major league manager were in Anaheim, San Diego, Montreal, and Seattle – none of which would exactly qualify as "east coast" cities. Finley sought to eliminate the threat of a Williams' departure by offering his manager a two-year contract extension, ostensibly locking in his services through the 1975 season. With the Williams question settled for the next two and a half years, Finley was once again quite comfortable in making life miserable for his manager.

Rise and Fall

Despite the contract extension, Williams continued to privately raise the possibility of leaving the Athletics after the 1973 season. As the season ended, signs of Williams' open defiance of Finley became visible, and Williams announced to his team in a closed-door meeting before World Series game three that he would not be back as their manager in 1974. Williams would later claim that the Mike Andrews incident had been the final straw, but the mounting tension between manager and owner and the desire on the part of a change by Williams made his departure inevitable. Williams' overt support for Andrews was a clear, public signal that he would not back down to Finley, setting the scene for some kind on confrontation. By this time Andrews was Public Enemy #1 in Finley's eyes, and it was very obvious that Williams was tweaking Finley with the move (Williams passed over Deron Johnson and Vic Davalillo, both superior hitters, to get Andrews into the game on the day of his reinstatement by Commissioner Bowie Kuhn).

And so it came as no surprise that once the Series was over, Dick Williams announced his intention to resign as manager of the Athletics, contract extension notwithstanding. If there was a surprise, it was the timing of the public announcement – Williams announced his plans on national television during the World Championship celebration in the Athletics' clubhouse while he and Finley were giving what was supposed to be the owner / manager celebratory joint interview for the national broadcast. Finley thanked Williams for his service "even though he won't be with us next year." Williams returned the thanks, but clearly stated that his decision to leave was final and would not be subject to reconsideration. In a formal press conference that followed a few

Help Wanted

minutes later, Williams again publicly announced his resignation. Williams took great pains to note not once but several times that the Andrews incident had no bearing on his decision, which he insisted had been reached well before the start of the series. When presented with a potential scenario that had Williams assume the role of manager of the New York Yankees, Williams stated that he would welcome that opportunity should it arise. As it turned out, the opportunity would arise and with it would come the next bizarre chapter in the Williams / Finley saga.

Unlike Charlie Finley, who employed eleven managers in his first eleven years as owner of the Athletics, the New York Yankees had been a model of relative stability at the managerial level. For the past twenty-five seasons, only four men had managed the Yankees. The incumbent in 1973 was Ralph Houk, a lifetime member of the Yankee organization currently on his second tour of duty as manager. Houk earned his early reputation as the brains behind the great Casey Stengel during the latter's final seasons as Yankee manager. He followed this with three seasons as Stengel's successor as manager, a period during which the Yankees lineup was blessed with one of the greatest assemblies of talent in the history of the game. As a reward for three American League Championships in his first three seasons as manager, Houk was promoted to the position of general manager. Houk was asked to return to the field leadership role a little more than a year into the reign of the ill-fated Johnny Keane in 1966. By this time the Yankees had suffered a complete collapse and it was the opinion of their management team that Houk was more valuable on the field than in an office. Houk proceeded to preside over eight seasons of the most lackluster performances in the storied history of the vaunted Yankee franchise. Houk demonstrated a laissez-faire style that served the team well when they were stocked with veteran superstars in the early sixties but was a disaster with the talent-poor Yankee teams of the late sixties and early seventies. As a result, the team fell into a pattern of mediocrity that lasted almost a decade. By 1973, the Yankees had been purchased by a syndicate led by the ambitious George Steinbrenner, who in turn brought in a new front-office team designed to break the pattern of losing that had become acceptable to the organization. The team was infused with a series of higher-quality ballplayers for 1973, and several pundits picked the Yankees to top the declining American League eastern division. After an early season run the team again fell in the standings, finishing fourth for the third consecutive year. Steinbrenner's soon to be famous impatience with managers that failed to deliver was driving him toward making a change, a move that was welcomed by Yankee fans that had turned viciously against Houk. Houk denied them all the pleasure of a firing, opting instead to resign on the final day of the season. What the Yankees now needed was someone who was Houk's opposite; a change agent, willing to break with tradition and do whatever was necessary to turn the team around and bring a championship to Yankee Stadium. Based on his record of delivering quick results by winning championships in his first seasons in both Boston and Oakland, Dick Williams was widely viewed as the turnaround specialist that the

Help Wanted

Yankees needed. This naturally led to the speculation that Williams was destined to be the next manager of the New York Yankees.

Before the courtship between the Yankees and Williams even got off the ground, Charles O. Finley made his presence in the matter felt by all involved. Despite the polite banter between Williams and Finley during the World Series celebration, Finley wasted no time making it clear to the Yankees that Dick Williams was under contract to the Oakland Athletics through 1975, resignation or no resignation. Finley astonished Yankee management when the annual league meetings began just a few short days after the World Series by announcing that Dick Williams wasn't going anywhere else to manage. Finley did make it clear that he would be willing to be more open-minded about Williams' future if he was appropriately compensated. The compensation he required was one or more of the Yankees' top stars, an absolute non-starter for Steinbrenner and his management team. Finley reduced his requirement – instead of Thurman Munson or some other top tier player, he would accept minor leaguers Otto Velez and Scott McGregor, the top two players in the Yankee farm system who were coveted by virtually every team in the major leagues; not a trade was discussed with Yankee management in which one or both of those names was not raised by the other organization. The Yankees again refused Finley's "offer", believing that they did not owe Finley any compensation, let alone two such valuable assets. The Yankees cited precedent, including the fact that Ralph Houk had recently resigned in the middle of a contract that locked him in through 1975, and yet the Yankees did not raise a single concern when Houk signed on to manage the Detroit Tigers a short time later. For his part, Finley also cited precedent, including the 1967 arrangement in which the New York Mets gave a large sum of cash and a player to the Washington Senators in return for an agreement by the Senators to release manager Gil Hodges from his contractual obligation so that he could be free to manage the Mets the following season. This time, neither team was willing to budge. The matter was submitted to the American League office for adjudication and both sides threatened legal action. By this time the Tigers were drawn into the controversy as the Yankees insisted that if Finley was going to hold Williams to his contract that the Yankees were within their rights to block Houk from managing anywhere else for the duration of his contract. In the midst of the controversy, the Yankees announced the signing of Williams as their new manager on December 13.

The Yankees began the Dick Williams era with a coming out party with the full New York press corps in attendance at Shea Stadium, the club's home for the upcoming season. Williams appeared in full Yankee regalia, expressing his enthusiasm for taking the reigns of the Yankees. In the meantime, the Athletics pushed their grievance with the American League office, charging the Yankees with "tampering" with Williams. The Yankees, in turn, lodged a similar action over Houk's arrangement with the Tigers. A week after the announcement of Williams as the new Yankee manager, American League President Joe Cronin, just days from retirement, announced his decision. After reviewing the facts, Cronin concluded that the Yankees and Houk had mutually agreed to terminate Houk's relationship with the team, including taking steps to terminate financial agreements that dated to

Help Wanted

Houk's days in the Yankee front office. Furthermore, Cronin noted that the Yankees had not objected to the Tigers hiring Houk until they themselves had received compensation demands from Finley. As a result, Cronin determined that the Yankees had no basis to hold Houk back from joining the Tigers and that the Yankees were not entitled to any compensation for their former manager.

In the case of Williams, Cronin determined that the pleasantries exchanged during the clubhouse celebration did not constitute an agreement by Finley to set Williams free to manage elsewhere and that Williams was bound to the Athletics for the duration of his extended contract. Any team that wished to employ Williams, including the Yankees, must reach a mutual agreement with Finley on compensation; otherwise Finley could effectively blacklist Williams for the next two seasons. Unwilling to part with Velez and McGregor and unable to get Finley to agree to an alternative arrangement, the frustrated Yankees were forced to give up their goal of hiring Williams. Bill Virdon was introduced as the new Yankee manager a short time later.

As for the Finley / Williams story, there was more to come. There was much conjecture whether Finley's motivation in restraining Williams was a vindictive attempt at retribution by Finley against Williams, a desire by Finley to annoy adversary George Steinbrenner, or a clear attempt to protect his assets. The answer is likely "all of the above." After forcing Williams to cool his heels as an executive in the insurance industry for the first half of 1974, Finley agreed to allow Williams to accept a position as manager of the California Angels.

Rise and Fall

Finley did not demand compensation in any form for the Angels, calling the release of Williams "an act of friendship" toward Angel owner Gene Autry. The professional relationship between Dick Williams and Charlie Finley was finally over.

None of these events addressed the immediate problem that Finley faced beginning that October evening – he still needed a field manager for 1974, and through all of the events following Williams' resignation, Williams insisted there was no way that it would be him. Days turned into weeks, and still the defending two-time World Champions had no manager, a condition that continued into mid-February. Rumors that field captain Sal Bando might assume the rare role of player-manager proved untrue. Finally, on February 20, a new manager was named. To the great surprise of all, the new manager of the Oakland Athletics would be none other than Alvin Dark, the very man Finley had fired less than seven years before.

Ironically, Dark had just finished riding out the remaining two and a half years on his multi-year contract with the Cleveland Indians, the team Dark joined after being fired from the Athletics and which had in turn fired him in 1971 after just short of four disappointing seasons as their manager. In recognition of the paradox he created by entrusting his championship team to the man he fired just a few years before, Finley told reporters at the Dark press conference "You'll want to know why I hired him. Well, there are several reasons. First of all, I know him a long time (sic). Yes, he managed the club before. Yes, he was fired. Yes, he's back. And yes, he expects to be fired again some day – all managers are eventually. But he told me he hopes it will be a helluva lot longer this time."

And so the strange story of who would manage the Athletics in 1974 came to an end. The manager fired for not backing Finley in 1967 would replace a manager that would not back Finley in 1973. Paradoxes aside, Alvin Dark would have just a few short days to prepare to take over one of the most turbulent positions imaginable with a very clear objective before him – to win a third consecutive World Championship.

Threepeat – Once More in '74

Convinced that the Athletics had the personnel that they needed to repeat again as World Champions and absorbed with the issues related to the managerial role, the Athletics stood pat during the winter trading season. The only deal of any importance was a trade that sent Horatio Pina to the Cubs in return for former Athletics' reliever Bob Locker. Second base was still considered to be the weak link in the lineup, but the team had won two World Championships with the bizarre rotation system at that position and there was no reason to expect that this approach would not work a third time. For the 1974 rotation, the Athletics planned to use rookie Manny Trillo in support of veterans Ted Kubiak and Dick Green, the latter having once again completed his off season ritual of retiring and returning to the fold.

The Athletics planned to reuse the same basic lineup from the prior season. The outfield of Joe Rudi, Billy North, and Reggie Jackson was arguably the game's best, and the club had confidence that 1973 newcomers Ray Fosse and Deron Johnson would continue to provide solid coverage in the catcher and designated hitter roles.

One offensive change the Athletics did make had to do with one of Charlie Finley's "specialty roles". Finley was a huge believer in the benefits of having a pinch running specialist on the bench. As early as the dark days of 1967, Finley had dedicated at least one precious spot on his twenty-five man roster to a running specialist. Finley's first designated speedster was Allan Lewis, known as the "Panamanian

Express" for his fleet-footedness. Although the switch-hitting outfielder hit as high as .319 in the minor leagues, Lewis was known more throughout his career as a base runner than as a hitter or fielder. The highlight of Lewis' base running career was his 116 stolen bases in the Florida State League in 1966. Lewis played parts of six seasons with the Athletics during the period of 1967-1973, playing in 156 regular-season games but making only thirty-one plate appearances and playing only ten times in the outfield, with the rest of his appearances coming as a pinch runner. By 1973 Lewis' teammates began to resent him and his specialty role, often publicly criticizing decisions to insert Lewis at the expense of one of the "complete players" on the team. The "designated runner" role of Lewis and the associated criticism was nothing compared to what would take place the following season.

For the 1974 season, Finley decided to turn his designated pinch runner program up a notch. At the very end of the 1974 spring training season Finley recruited Herb Washington, a world-class sprinter who had won an NCAA championship and had set world records in both the 50 and 60-yard dash. In the early 1970's, competitive track and field athletes performed under an incredibly oppressive amateur code that prohibited them from accepting compensation of any kind based upon anything even remotely related to their athletic activities. By signing with the Athletics, Washington was writing off any future amateur track career he might still have. Although Washington was listed on the roster as an outfielder, everyone, including Washington, knew that was a joke. Washington had never really played organized baseball, and he made no effort while with the Athletics to focus on any baseball skills except base running. While the team went through pre-game hitting and fielding drills, Washington went through a typical sprinters program of stretching and calisthenics. When the season began, the great sprinter experiment was put into effect. Washington quickly learned what his critics already knew – it takes a lot more than blazing speed to be a great base stealer. In his April 4 debut he distracted pitcher Steve Hargan enough to force a wild pitch. That would be the highlight of his first weeks as a major leaguer. Three days later he was caught leaning by Jim Merritt; Washington continued on to second base, where he was tagged out for his first "caught stealing". In fairness to Washington, his lack of baseball experience, coupled with virtually no spring training, forced him into an "on the job training" situation at the major league level – a very tough classroom. A week later he successfully stole his first base. That would be his only stolen base until the 25th of May, when he was credited with a steal as part of the back end of a double steal. In his efforts to please Finley, manager Dark continued to diligently use Washington as a pinch runner, despite his relative lack of success in energizing the offense. The steal on the 25th seemed to mark a transition point at which Washington became more comfortable with reading pitchers; after that day Washington's base running productivity improved dramatically. Washington's base stealing form was still a bit raw. His slid awkwardly, always head first to avoid any potential injuries to his precious legs. He was still picked off at an abnormally high rate, but in many cases he was fast enough to make it to second ahead of the relay throw from the first baseman. Most importantly, Washington began scoring runs in June. But Washington's performance was really a sideshow with little material impact on the Athletics' ability to win games, although manager Alvin

Dark would later credit Washington with making a major contribution to eight Athletic victories. Still, the box scores tell a different story, and most of Washington's appearances had little impact on helping the Athletics win close games; contributions like his stolen base and run scored in an Athletics' one-run win on August 2 were an anomaly. Washington made the ultimate attempt to make a difference as base stealer on September 25 by attempting to steal home against Bert Blyleven and the Minnesota Twins, an attempt that was unsuccessful. Washington ended the season with twenty-nine runs scored and twenty-nine stolen bases with sixteen unsuccessful steal attempts, all in ninety-two pinch running appearances. In the process he absorbed an important roster spot that could have been used by a player that could have contributed in some other way.

The Athletics' 1974 starting pitching staff again boasted three of the top pitchers in the league in Catfish Hunter, Ken Holtzman, and Vida Blue. But once again there was a startling lack of depth behind the big three. Behind the trio of stars, the Athletics had young Dave Hamilton and veteran Blue Moon Odom, each of whom performed admirably but neither earned the full confidence of manager Alvin Dark. As a result, Hunter, Holtzman, and Blue piled on the starts and the innings, with Hamilton and Odom filling in whenever the three key starters were absolutely unavailable. The team survived a potentially devastating blow when Blue was briefly hospitalized for chest pains during the season. Tests on the young pitcher's heart showed no signs of problems and Blue quickly returned to the rotation.

Rise and Fall

The Athletics started the 1974 season looking like anything but the dominant team in the American League. For the first month of the season they failed to win more than two games in a row and by May 7 they found themselves three games under .500 and in fifth place in a relatively weak American League western division. As a sign of the weakened state of the division, a five game winning streak by the Athletics launched the defending champions back into first place. Despite the return to the top of the division, the pressure on the Athletics and the team's relatively poor performance took its toll. The lightning rod for the frustration that boiled over in the Athletics' clubhouse was manager Alvin Dark. Dark had drawn the ire of virtually every player on the team through what many considered a non-stop series of bizarre player moves during early season games, many of which involved the insertion of pinch runner Washington. It soon seemed like every player move made by Dark drew some form of criticism by the players involved, often in the form of a public comment or display of emotion. Dark's pitchers were particularly vocal about the quick hook that Dark often used. The outspoken Ken Holtzman expressed the feelings of his fellow starters when he proclaimed, "the only twenty-game winners we are going to have this year are (relief pitchers) Rollie Fingers and Darold Knowles." The pitchers were also furious with Dark's practice of calling pitches from the bench. The hurlers countered with small acts of defiance – Fingers once de facto overruled Dark's decision not to intentionally walk a hitter by purposefully throwing four straight pitches out of the strike zone. Dark later commented that the situation was made worse by sportswriters feeding off of the players' attitudes, which in turn fueled the emotions of the fans, creating an untenable atmosphere for the manager. Rather than supporting his manager, owner Finley piled on. Finley publicly criticized Dark for being "too soft" on the players and often ripped the manager while in the presence of both press and players. Dark's coaches did not make his life any easier; in fact, Dark believed that coach Vern Hoscheit was undermining his managerial authority by going behind his back to complain to Finley about Dark's decisions. The situation hit rock bottom when team captain Sal Bando exploded after one frustrating loss. While venting his frustration, Bando proclaimed that Dark "could not manage a meat market." The third baseman did not know that his manager was just a few feet away at the time. The deeply sensitive Dark was devastated by Bando's comment, and Bando himself was terribly embarrassed by the incident. Ironically, the outrageousness of incidents like this eventually opened the eyes of the players and their captain, and it was Bando himself who soon called for players to end their public criticisms of Dark and focus on the task as hand – winning their fourth consecutive divisional championship. Clubhouse leader Catfish Hunter later commented that the torrent of criticism against Dark, particularly that which came from Finley, eventually served to rally the players in support of the besieged manager; Hunter later proclaimed that the eventual 1974 championship was dedicated to Dark.

The Athletics never enjoyed an overwhelming hot streak through the early part of the season, but they continued to play just well enough that they were never really threatened for the top spot in the standings. As a sign of the future, the Athletics' closest nemesis throughout the early part of the season was the Kansas City Royals. The Royals stayed within striking distance of the Athletics through much of the season and were as close as four games back on August 25. But at that point the Royals imploded as they went 9-27 for the remainder of the season. The Athletics maintained their steady play, and no other team filled the void opened by the decline of the Royals. As a result, the Athletics marched along to their fourth consecutive first place finish, ending the season five games ahead of the second place Texas Rangers. Despite the relative ease with which the club won their division, it was a source of concern for all involved that their .556 winning percentage was the team's lowest since their second place finish in 1970. It was in fact the fourth consecutive season that the Athletics' winning percentage had declined, a very alarming trend indeed.

While criticism of Dark was suppressed, disharmony in the clubhouse between the ballplayers themselves, long a trademark of the Athletics, boiled to a point unseen since the meltdown of 1967. The situation hit bottom in June when outfielders Billy North and Reggie Jackson, each burdened with an intense dislike of the other, came to blows in a violent clubhouse fight in early June. Catcher Ray Fosse tried to separate the two and was badly injured in the process. While North and Jackson were pressured by owner Finley to put the matter behind them, Fosse would bear the result of the fight in a terrible way. Unable to play in the days following the brawl, Fosse was eventually required to undergo surgery to replace a disc ruptured in the fight. Fosse was out of the lineup until late August, and his offensive productivity, which had been disappointing to begin with, fell to virtually nothing. Fosse ended the season with a paltry .196 batting average.

Threepeat – Once More in '74

The Athletics' slide was further reflected in the performances of several of their other key players. Deron Johnson's offensive rebirth in 1973 proved to be nothing more than an analogy of a light bulb burning brighter just before it burns out; a thumb injury had resulted in Johnson's bat losing much of the pop it had carried through most of his fourteen years in the major leagues. With Johnson's average falling below the .200 level, the Athletics chose to send him to the Milwaukee Brewers in a June trade. Gene Tenace also saw his batting average plummet, although he was hitting home runs at a healthy clip. Dick Green suffered from a series of nagging injuries, driving him from the lineup for several weeks.

Through it all, Dark managed to piece together a daily lineup that managed to win just enough to keep the team at the top of the standings. Dark called upon the venerable Ted Kubiak and young Manny Trillo to replace Green. Replacing Fosse would not be as easy. Gene Tenace was moved from first base back behind the plate, but a pinched nerve sapped his already weak defensive contribution. In desperation, Dark called upon veteran backup catcher Larry Haney to help fill the gap, but Haney's anemic bat contributed only a .165 average and 3 RBI in over 70 games. Pat Bourque also filled in at first base, but like many of his counterparts he was unable to contribute offensively. Angel Mangual, his position with the Athletics saved by the departure of Dick Williams, became Deron Johnson's primary replacement at designated hitter, but he was generally unsuited for fueling the offensive engine.

Rise and Fall

When faced with roster challenges similar to what they were suffering in 1974, the Athletics had historically turned to the waiver wire. In 1974 they took a page from the earlier days of Finley's regime by looking to their own minor league system – deep in that system. To stabilize their deteriorating offense, the Athletics promoted nineteen year-old Claudell Washington from Birmingham in the double-A Southern League. Washington had been terrorizing Southern League pitching, and the Athletics chose to take a gamble on the young outfielder. In his first start as the team's new designated hitter, Washington broke up a highly publicized fifteen game winning streak by Cleveland's Gaylord Perry with a game winning single in the bottom of the tenth. Although he did not show any power, Washington contributed many timely hits in the latter half of the season. His insertion as designated hitter also allowed Angel Mangual to return to the outfield, freeing Joe Rudi to move to first base to replace Tenace. Claudell Washington's arrival was a key milestone in the Athletics' drive for their fourth straight divisional crown.

It wasn't a very pretty season for the Athletics. The team's trademark friction, players with players, the players with the manager, and Finley with everybody, seemed to truly impede the team's performance on the field. The club had almost become a self-parody. In a division with more robust competition, the club may have had difficulty repeating as divisional champions. But great teams overcome adversity, and time and again the Athletics found a way to win. And,

Threepeat – Once More in '74

much to the chagrin of the team's many, many critics, the Athletics were a great team. But for the "Fighting A's" the job wasn't done until they had battled their way to a third consecutive World Championship.

Ruthless Efficiency

For the third time in four years the Athletics would face the Baltimore Orioles in their quest for the League Championship. The Orioles featured virtually the same cast as they had during the previous season's loss to the Athletics in the League Championship Series. The Orioles had faced an unexpected challenge from the resurgent New York Yankees that forced them to fight for the divisional title right up to the final days of the season. In a turnabout from the previous year, revenge was now the Orioles' mission.

For the second time in three years, Reggie Jackson's hamstring would be a factor in the post-season. Jackson injured his leg in the closing days of the regular season and would be forced into the role of designated hitter through most of the playoffs. A thin bench and a day-to-day status for Jackson were not elements that favored the Athletics as the series began.

Once again the League Championship Series did not begin well for the Athletics. Catfish Hunter, prone to throwing a gopher ball, gave up three home runs to the Orioles in the first game before yielding the mound and a 6-1 deficit to Blue Moon Odom in the fifth inning. It would be the earliest exit for Hunter in twelve post-season starts with the Athletics. The Athletics characteristically fought back, but still lost by a 6-3 score.

Ruthless Efficiency

Game two was a completely different story from the opener. Athletic starter Ken Holtzman shut the Oriole bats down completely, scattering five singles in the course of throwing a 5-0 shutout. Sal Bando got the offensive show started with a solo home run, and a homer by Ray Fosse in the bottom of the eighth capped off a three run rally that sealed the victory. The best-of-five series moved to Baltimore for its conclusion.

Game three featured the finest post-season performance of Vida Blue's career. Blue was on his game as he held the Orioles to two hits without giving up a single walk. Oriole ace Jim Palmer was almost as good, but not good enough. Palmer made a single mistake, resulting in a Sal Bando fourth inning home run. With Blue pitching so well, it was the only run the Athletics would need.

In game four, Catfish Hunter nearly duplicated Blue's performance, taking a two-hitter into the eighth inning. Though they had yet to record their first hit of the game, the Athletics took the lead in the fifth inning by scoring on four walks issues by Oriole pitcher Mike Cuellar, who would walk an amazing total of nine Athletics in less than five innings of work. Reliever Ross Grimsley continued to hold the Athletics hitless into the seventh inning, when Sal Bando walked and was driven home with the go-ahead run courtesy of a Reggie Jackson double. When Hunter gave up a leadoff single in the Oriole half of the eighth, Alvin Dark called on super reliever Rollie Fingers to try to save the game. Fingers shut the Orioles down in the eighth, making it thirty innings without a run scored by Baltimore. Matters grew serious for the

Rise and Fall

Athletics in the bottom of the ninth, as the Orioles finally pushed a run across the plate and managed to get the tying run into scoring position and the potential winning run on first with two outs. Dark stayed with ace reliever Fingers, and Fingers rewarded his skipper's confidence by striking out Don Baylor to ice the game and the team's third consecutive League Championship title. Only one hurdle remained between the Athletics and the baseball immortality guaranteed by winning a third consecutive World Series – the National League Champion Los Angeles Dodgers.

The 1974 World Series marked a first in the history of the fall classic. The World Series first arrived on the west coast courtesy of the Los Angeles Dodgers in 1959. Since then, the Series had been played in California six times, but each time the local team had faced a challenger from the eastern or central regions of the country. For the first time, the 1974 Series would feature two California teams. Dubbed the "freeway series" in a tip of the cap to the "subway series" that celebrated the baseball dominance of the city of New York for so long, the 1974 Series signaled a symbolic shift in baseball's power center from the east to the west coast.

As the Athletics worked out in Dodger Stadium in preparation for the second defense of their world title, tempers once again flared in the team's clubhouse. This time it was pitchers Rollie Fingers and Blue Moon Odom that engaged in physical combat. Fingers cut his head on a locker, resulting in five stitches in the scalp of the relief ace. As painful as that may have been, it was Odom that initially appeared to be the more seriously injured; an ankle injury rendered the right-hander "day-to-day" for the Series. Also day-to-day was Reggie Jackson, the heart of the club's offensive attack. A sore hamstring had plagued Jackson throughout the League Championship Series; as the World Series opened Jackson was available for play in the field, but the knowledge that his fragile hamstring could give out at any time hung over him and the team.

Concerns over Jackson's health were eased somewhat in the top of the second inning of game one when the slugger hit the second of what would be ten World Series home runs that he would hit during his illustrious career. As they had all season, the Athletics overcame adversity and employed a combination of skill and creativity to score a game one victory over the hometown Dodgers. A fifth inning double by pitcher Ken Holtzman was followed by a wild pitch and a perfectly executed squeeze bunt by Bert Campaneris to score the team's second run. Holtzman fell victim to Alvin Dark's quick hook in the bottom of that inning when Rollie Fingers entered the game to squelch a Dodger rally which pushed across a run to make the score 2-1. The Athletics manufactured a third run in the eighth courtesy of a single, a bunt, and an error to make the score 3-1. The durable Fingers pitched into the ninth inning, retiring the first two Dodgers without incident before a Jim Wynn home run made things interesting. When Steve Garvey followed with a single, Dark decided he had to make a move. With his ace righty reliever already used up and the dangerous right-handed hitter Joe Ferguson due up, Dark again had to improvise. His emergency choice as a stopper was Catfish Hunter. Hunter struck out Ferguson, sealing the victory and earning his first and only post-season save. Once again, the Athletics had found a way to manufacture a win against less than desirable circumstances.

No such redemption would befall the Athletics in game two. Los Angeles built a 3-0 lead against Vida Blue, while future Hall of Famer Don Sutton held the Athletics to just two hits through seven innings. The Athletics loaded the bases in the eighth but were uncharacteristically prevented from pushing a run across the plate. A hit batsman and a Reggie Jackson double to start the ninth finally drove Sutton from the mound. Joe Rudi greeted reliever Mike Marshall with a two-run single to make the score 3-2. Following the pattern used throughout the 1974 regular season, Dark substituted Herb Washington for the relatively slow-footed Rudi as the runner at first base. Washington had been utilized twice in the League Championship Series and was caught trying to steal second base each time, an inauspicious post-season start to be sure. Marshall possessed an extremely effective pickoff move, particularly for a right-hander. He toyed with Washington, stepping off the rubber several times to force the sprinter to dive back to the bag. Each time, Washington bravely increased his lead, straining to take off in response to the steal sign flashed by Dark. A snap pickoff throw from Marshall caught the "designated runner" leaning, and Washington was caught diving back to the bag. As the embarrassed speedster disappeared into the Athletics' dugout, the Athletics' comeback disappeared with him. Marshall closed the game and the Series was tied at a game apiece.

As veterans of two consecutive pressure filled, seven-game World Series, the Athletics took the game two loss in stride. The Athletics got on the scoreboard first in game three, again by playing "small ball". Billy North reached first on a single, then sprinted all the way to third on a simple ground out. A walk and a subsequent error gave the Athletics a 1-0 lead. A Joe Rudi single increased the lead to 2-0. The Athletics manufactured another run in the fourth behind a walk, a bunt, and a single. While the Athletics scrapped for runs, Catfish Hunter meticulously handled the Dodger hitters, holding them scoreless until Bill Buckner homered in the top of the eighth. Further damage was avoided when Dick Green snagged a blistering line drive off the bat of Steve Garvey and doubled Jim Wynn off of first base to extinguish a Dodger rally. It was the second line drive that Green had turned into a double play in the game. Herb Washington made his second appearance of the Series in the Athletics' half of the eighth inning; again the sprinter made a simple base running mistake. With two outs, Dick Green flied to left field. Washington quickly scampered to second, then stood there watching Bill Buckner catch the final out of the inning rather than running on to third. Had the ball fallen in it would have been yet another base running embarrassment for the besieged pinch runner. The Dodgers gave the Athletics a scare in the ninth when Willie Crawford, the high schooler who a decade earlier had snubbed Charlie Finley's lucrative offer to sign with the Athletics, led off with a home run off of Rollie Fingers. An error by Bert Campaneris put the tying run on first before it was erased by a game-ending double play initiated by Dick Green. It was the third twin killing initiated by Green during the game, a World Series record for the slick-fielding infielder. Ironically, Green followed a brilliant day in the field for the Athletics by repeating his frequent criticism of the Oakland Coliseum's infield, calling it the worst playing surface in the American League.

While the Athletics had taken the lead in the Series, the National League challengers were far from impressed with the scrappy defending champs. Bill Buckner was quoted in a San Francisco newspaper as disparaging the Athletics' players and having compared the Athletics to the San Diego Padres. For the record, the Padres lost over one hundred games in 1974, finishing at the bottom of their division, forty-two games behind the Dodgers. Buckner had unwittingly ignited the Athletics, a club used to turning their emotions toward each other rather than the opposition. It was a move that Buckner would soon have cause to regret.

While the Athletics passions may have been fanned by Buckner's comments, their bats were still cool in the first half of game four. Pitcher Ken Holtzman provided the only early fireworks with a solo home run in the third inning. Holtzman owned a lifetime World Series batting average of .333 with three doubles and a home run in twelve Series at bats. The Dodgers answered back with two runs in the fourth to take a 2-1 lead. The Athletics took the lead for good in the bottom of the sixth. Again, the club had to scrape their way through a four-run rally that consisted of three walks, two singles, an error and a sacrifice bunt. Regardless of the method, the team had earned a 5-2 lead,

Ruthless Efficiency

a lead that Holtzman and reliever Rollie Fingers held to clinch the victory. Dick Green once again closed the game with a diving stop that led to another sensational double play.

The Athletics opened game five with what was becoming a typical Athletics' World Series rally – a single, a stolen base, a throwing error, and a sacrifice fly. Light-hitting Ray Fosse contributed to the lead with a second inning home run. Another defensive gem by Dick Green, this time an outstanding relay throw to nab a Dodger base runner in the third inning, snuffed an important Dodger rally before damage could be done. The Dodgers did finally tie the game 2-2 in the sixth inning, setting up a dramatic conclusion. In the bottom of the seventh, unruly Oakland fans began showering the playing field with litter when the Dodgers took the field. The game was delayed for six minutes while stadium security regained control of the crowd and the field was cleared. Dodger pitcher Mike Marshall passed the time during the delay not by throwing warm-up pitches, but by conversing with the umpire crew. Marshall was an expert in human kinetics, the science of how the human body moves. The enigmatic Marshall eventually earned a Ph.D. in the subject. Marshall applied his expertise in kinesiology to the art of pitching, setting a record by appearing in 106 games in 1974, including a record stretch of thirteen consecutive games. Marshall believed that he knew his body, including when he needed warm-up pitches. In opting to forego additional warm-ups during the extended delay, Marshall may have made a mistake that would prove to be fatal to the Dodgers World Series dreams. The very first pitch by Marshall after the interruption was drilled into the seats by leadoff hitter Joe Rudi, giving the Athletics a 3-2 lead. Rollie Fingers came into the game to seal the victory with his second save of the Series.

While the 1974 World Series did not match the drama of the previous two, seven-game series won by the Athletics, and while the club was forced to scratch for most of the runs they scored in their victories, the achievement of a third consecutive world title was nonetheless a sweet one for the ballclub. Emblematic of the club's victory was the selection of second baseman Dick Green as the recipient of the Babe Ruth Award for the most outstanding Series performance. The recognition to Green was a tribute to his outstanding defensive play against the Dodgers. In fact, Green had gone hitless in thirteen Series at bats, dropping his career post-season batting average to a paltry .155. But Green proved again in the Series that his importance to the team went way beyond his offensive contribution. Unfortunately, the 1974 World Series would signal the end of an era as Green wore the Athletic uniform for the very last time. The one Athletic player that had joined the organization prior to the arrival of Charlie Finley, the true first seed of the Athletics' dynasty, would retire for good that winter.

For the Oakland Athletics, their history making three consecutive World Championships should have been a cause for unbridled joy and celebration. They were the undisputed kings of baseball, and their roster was full of players who were in the very prime of their careers. Nobody could blame the Athletics if they confidently looked forward to many more years of dominating their competition. But there was a dark cloud forming over the ballclub. It started with a rumor and a whisper, a portrait of a scenario of incredible and unbelievable proportion. The story first broke in a big way during the World Series and took off after its completion. If it was true it could have disastrous consequences on the Athletics' prospects for future championships.

According to the stories circulating that October, there was a legitimate possibility that Catfish Hunter would be leaving the Athletics.

A technicality involving payments due to Hunter under a complicated contract provision could make Hunter a free agent. As shocking and unbelievable as it was, the Oakland Athletics were on the brink of losing the very foundation of their pitching staff, jeopardizing the roster stability upon which they had built three consecutive World Championships.

First Exit

Rumors of an extraordinary contract issue between Charlie Finley and Catfish Hunter began circulating in earnest during the World Series. What Finley called "just a little misunderstanding" soon blossomed into one of the most remarkable incidents in the history of baseball.

Catfish Hunter's 1974 contract was not the typical agreement signed by players of that era. The $100,000 total value of the contract was commensurate with Hunter's performance and his stature as one of the best pitchers in the game. What was unusual about the contract was the manner in which the $100,000 would be paid to Hunter. At Hunter's request, $50,000 would be paid throughout the season as regular salary and the remaining $50,000 would be paid into a tax deferred insurance annuity. Finley agreed to the deal, going so far as to stipulating specific wording regarding the annuity in the contract itself. As the season progressed, Hunter received his regular salary payments but noticed that the annuity payments were never made. When the payments were still unpaid at mid-season, Hunter's attorney sent a formal letter to Finley stating that he was in default on his contract. Still the payments were not made. By this time Finley was overtly balking at making any deferred payments, offering to pay the remaining $50,000 as conventional salary. Finley claimed that an annuity payment, unlike a salary payment, could not be classified as a business expense by the club and would therefore have tax ramifications for the cash-conscious Finley. But an additional

First Exit

salary payment was not what Hunter wanted, nor was it what the contract stipulated.

The parties began to meet to attempt to resolve the dispute under the facilitation of baseball Commissioner Bowie Kuhn and American League President Lee MacPhail. Finley expressed bewilderment over the conflict, claiming that he had not defaulted on the contract and publicly repeating his offer of paying Hunter $50,000 in cash as a salary payment. MacPhail reported to the press that Finley's offer effectively put the matter to rest. But Hunter would not budge – he was adamant that Finley abide by the terms specified in his contract.

Upon the conclusion of the season, Hunter engaged the services of the Major League Baseball Players Association counsel, Dick Moss, to initiate formal grievance procedures against Finley. The charge was breach of contract. The remedy requested by Hunter and the MLBPA – payment of the delinquent annuity funds (plus a penalty) and free agency for Hunter. The Hunter camp's argument was that no player should be forced to play for an owner who had blatantly breached a legal contract that was signed in good faith. Finley and Commissioner Bowie Kuhn tried to evade the MLBPA and address the grievance privately, but Hunter and the MLBPA insisted that the formal procedures be followed. These procedures stipulated that such grievances be heard by a three man panel consisting of an MLBPA representative, an owner's representative, and a third party, a truly independent labor arbitrator. The arbitrator assigned to hear the grievance was Peter Seitz, the same Peter Seitz that would turn the game of baseball upside down a year later in the McNally / Messersmith case.

The Hunter hearing took place on November 26 at the MLBPA offices. The arbitration panel reviewed the contract and took testimony from Hunter, Finley, and their respective legal teams. Finley testified that regardless of what Hunter's contract (which Finley himself had signed) said, he was completely unaware of any agreement to defer half of the compensation. Seitz clearly found Finley's "explanation" completely unacceptable and saw it for what it was worth – a lie.

December 16, 1974 was a major milestone in the history of baseball and, most importantly, in the history of the Oakland Athletics. On that day, the arbitration panel announced their decision. Charlie Finley would be required to make the agreed-to annuity payments and pay a penalty to cover the lost interest on the account. That settled the matter of the withheld payments. But Hunter's real coup d'état was his new status as a free agent; Hunter would not be forced to work another day for an owner that had breached his contract. The Athletics would have no recourse, even if they agreed to meet or exceed an offer by another club the final decision on where to play would be Hunter's. Finley eventually appealed all the way to the California Supreme Court, but saw his appeals struck down at every level. Catfish Hunter was a free agent.

In the aftermath of the panel's decision, Bowie Kuhn called for a moratorium on any negotiations between Hunter and potential new teams

First Exit

until he could assess the findings. A cynic might suggest that Kuhn was caught in a very difficult position; on one hand, the Commissioner recognized the danger that free agents posed to the status quo of baseball. After all, the Commissioner was hired by and served at the pleasure of the owners, and at that time the owners had a clear economic incentive to squash any movement toward free agency, even in exceptional circumstances such as this. On the other hand, the enmity between Kuhn and Finley was well known and this was clearly a significant personal defeat for the Athletics' owner. After two days of reflection, Kuhn ended his moratorium. For the second time in seven years, there would be a marquee player on the free agent market, courtesy of Charlie Finley.

The bidding for Hunter's services began immediately. With a newly awarded Cy Young award in Hunter's possession to validate what everyone already knew (that Catfish Hunter was the very best pitcher in the American League), it was clear from the start that the bidding war for Hunter would make the earlier competition to sign Ken Harrelson pale in comparison. Hunter was viewed as a franchise player that could make a mediocre team a contender and a contending team a champion. Hunter entered the process with high hopes, but even his wildest expectations were quickly eclipsed as the big money owners made their desire to secure Hunter's services known. In the end it was the New York Yankees that landed the prize fish, turning the Catfish into a goldfish with a guaranteed contract of $3.48 million (much of it deferred!).

For the Yankees, 1974 had been turnaround year. They had set aside years of being a bystander in the American League east pennant races to come from nowhere to finish within two games of the first place Orioles. To them, Catfish Hunter meant twenty wins in the bank and a probable trip to their first post-season in a decade. Hunter would also be the cornerstone of a marketing program that heralded the return to greatness in the Bronx.

For the Oakland Athletics, it was a very different story indeed. While the Yankees celebrated, Finley seethed. Finley never accepted anything regarding the Hunter situation – not his obligation to defer half of Hunter's salary, not the authority of the arbitration panel, and not even the final decision, which Finley confidently but incorrectly believed would be overturned in the courts (it wasn't). Meanwhile, the majority of Athletics' players hated Finley and envied Hunter for his newfound freedom. They also recognized that New York's gain of a certain twenty victories meant a corresponding loss for the Athletics.

Worse still, the core team that Charlie Finley had so painstakingly assembled was starting to fall apart. The Oakland Athletics had lost their heart and soul when Catfish Hunter walked away, and the team would never be the same.

While the Hunter case would stand temporarily as a one-time event in the history of baseball free agency, it was not the only threat to the Athletics' roster. In April 1974, the formation of the World Baseball Association was announced. The WBA was to be a thirty-two-team league with franchises located throughout the world. They possessed an

First Exit

entrepreneurial spirit that in other circumstances would have made Charlie Finley proud, with a set of rules that included:

- Five designated hitters and a designated runner in every lineup

- A twenty-second limit between pitches

- Three ball walks and fluorescent orange baseballs (long-standing Finley ideas)

- Two runs credited for stealing home after the sixth inning

To stock their rosters, WBA organizers lustfully eyed the staff of existing major league teams. League officials claimed to have engaged in negotiations with dozens of established major league players, including six members of Charlie Finley's Athletics. Rumored to be among those being courted by the WBA was Athletic captain Sal Bando. If true, this would have ruined the Athletics. As it turned out the WBA never got off the ground. There would be no mass defection from the Athletics.

The reprieve, however, was only temporary.

Hollow Victory

The A's three consecutive World Championships landed them in elite company in the history of baseball. It was a feat that was surpassed only by the New York Yankee teams of 1936-1939 and 1949-1953. To win three consecutive championships required a rare combination of great talent, consistent play, stability, a healthy dose of luck, and good timing in the form of an absence of a significantly overwhelming opponent.

Even with the departure of Catfish Hunter, the 1975 Athletics still had an abundance of great talent and were well positioned to "Keep it Alive in 75", the new public relations motto for the team. The collection of youngsters assembled by Charlie Finley so many years ago had now matured into a group of seasoned veterans, tempered by pennant races, post-season pressure, and the ongoing distraction of Finley's non-stop side show. The club's depth enabled them to weather extended losing streaks and facilitated the level of consistent play required to survive over the long haul of a 162 game regular season and the unforgiving nature of a short, post-season series. Until the loss of Hunter, the club had maintained a remarkable record of holding on to their top players – the Athletics never seemed to make a bad player move. And the club was fortunate to hit their peak at a time when there was an absence of significant competition in the American League western division. Although different teams had mounted a challenge to the Athletics' supremacy at various times during their run, no team was

Hollow Victory

able to assemble an arsenal of strong players similar to that which Oakland had built during their formative years.

The largest single threat to the A's mission to capture a fifth straight divisional title and a fourth consecutive World Championship was the void left by the loss of Catfish Hunter. Hunter's leadership would be missed at least as much as his twenty-five victories. The Athletics' pitching staff had relied heavily on the Hunter-Blue-Holtzman triumvirate, with each pitcher starting close to forty games per season as well as playing critical roles in the post-season. At the age of thirty, Blue Moon Odom was but a shadow of the successful pitcher he had been just a few seasons before. Dave Hamilton and Glenn Abbott were solid major leaguers, but hardly of the caliber of the young Athletics' pitchers of the late 1960's. Neither pitcher ever seemed to earn the confidence of Athletics' management. Hamilton later commented publicly that the Athletics had failed to handle either pitcher properly during their time with the team, noting that whenever they gave up a couple of hits in the first or second inning of a game they would see immediate action in their bullpen while other starters were not subjected to that kind of pressure. Try as they might, the Athletics were unable to acquire a pitcher to compensate for Hunter; they would face the opening of the 1975 season with a patchwork rotation built around the remaining staff anchors, Ken Holtzman and Vida Blue.

Confident that young Claudell Washington was now ready to tackle the role of everyday left fielder, the Athletics now had options for addressing the remaining holes in their lineup. In a controversial move,

Rise and Fall

Finley and Alvin Dark chose to relocate Joe Rudi, arguably the best left fielder in the American League, to first base on a full-time basis. It was not a move that made Rudi happy; he publicly suggested that Reggie Jackson, with his increasingly delicate legs, might be a more appropriate choice to move to first. The Rudi move freed up Gene Tenace, who in turn replaced Ray Fosse as the everyday catcher. As was the case with Rudi, Tenace's relocation back to the catcher's spot made drew a negative public reaction from the player. Tenace, unhappy with recent salary negotiations, had responded that he was no longer interested in playing the more rigorous catcher's position and that he wanted to be traded away from the defending champions. Nevertheless, Tenace found himself as the Athletics' regular catcher as the season opened.

Dick Green's annual retirement at the completion of the 1974 campaign was different from his prior attempts to leave the game behind – this one was permanent. Green sought to break the regular patter by agreeing to come back, but only for an enormous salary. Contributing to Green's commitment to making this his final retirement was his public proclamation that the Athletics could not repeat as champions without Catfish Hunter. With the full realization that he was asking for more pay than he was worth, Green had finally found a way to make his final exit from the game. With Green now permanently retired, the starting second base job was now open. None of Green's backups appeared to be natural successors at the position. Rookie Phil Garner eventually emerged as the opening day second baseman. Garner was a transplanted third baseman, but he proved to be a quick study and a durable second sacker.

Hollow Victory

The lone remaining gap left over from the 1974 lineup was the designated hitter role. Since the decline and departure of Deron Johnson, the designated hitter role had been problematic for the Athletics. Claudell Washington had done an admirable job in the role, but he was short on power and the designated hitter role was no place for a well-rounded young talent like Washington. For the first two years that the designated hitter role had been in existence, the Athletics had largely relied on stopgaps, players that opportunistically filled the role on a temporary basis. 1975 would be different. Less than a week after the end of the 1974 World Series, Finley turned to his frequent trading partner, the Chicago Cubs, for his new designated hitter. In the fifth major trade completed with the Cubs in recent years, Finley acquired aging superstar Billy Williams in exchange for the injured Bob Locker, who had missed the entire 1974 season, backup infielder Manny Trillo, and bullpen ace Darold Knowles. The Cubs were rebuilding and were in the process of divesting their highly paid veteran players. The thirty-seven year-old Williams was the stereotypical designated hitter – an aging slugger, eager to extend his career by avoiding the daily strain of playing in the field. The acquisition of Williams was considered to be one of the greatest coups in modern Athletic history, and Finley greeted his new star with a $200,000 annual salary. With the acquisition of Williams, the maturation of Washington, and the arrival of Garner, the Athletics had good reason to be optimistic about the productivity of their lineup in 1975. The final piece of the puzzle also came courtesy of the Cubs with the arrival of Jim Todd, who was destined to round out the Athletics' bullpen.

Rise and Fall

The Athletics were once again the league leaders in salary arbitration cases in the spring of 1975. Thirteen Athletics filed for arbitration, but seven settled before the arbitration board heard their cases. Of the sixteen total cases eventually heard by the salary arbiters in 1975, six were Athletics. Rollie Fingers and Ted Kubiak won their cases, while Reggie Jackson, Ken Holtzman, Sal Bando, and Ray Fosse all lost. The bad blood generated by the process, particularly among the superstars that had lost their cases, continued to build.

When the club broke spring camp in preparation to head home for the season opener they believed they had solved at least part of their starting pitching quandary. The solution came from a most unlikely source in the presence of a twenty year-old rookie named Mike Norris. Norris made the squad on the basis of a strong spring with the hope that he might be the 1975 version of Vida Blue. In his major league debut he created a stir by shutting out the Chicago White Sox on just three hits. He proved that this was no fluke by limiting the Kansas City Royals to a single hit in seven innings in his next start. If the Norris story seemed too good to be true, it was. Norris left his third start with an elbow injury after facing a single batter – his season was essentially ended by subsequent surgery and the Athletics' starting pitching woes appeared more dire than before. As Blue Moon Odom appeared to have lost his ability be to get hitters out, Glenn Abbott and Dave Hamilton were called on to fill the gap.

Hollow Victory

Despite their lack of starting pitching depth, the Athletics got off to a strong start in April. At month's end they were once again in their familiar position atop the western division standings. Billy Williams' bat appeared to have lost some pop, and in mid-May the aging star's batting average hovered slightly above the .200 mark. Fortunately, Claudell Washington proved his successful rookie season was an accurate reflection of his ability and he continued to hit for a high average. In early May, the Herb Washington experiment officially ended. The speedster's fate was sealed in the spring when the Athletics acquired Don Hopkins from the Montreal Expos. Unlike Herb Washington, Hopkins was a true baseball player, capable of playing in the field. Washington appeared in just thirteen early season games in 1975 with only two successful steals in three attempts. Unable to justify maintaining two running specialists on the roster, Finley chose to dedicate the pinch runner role to the more versatile Hopkins.

After the first few weeks of the 1975 season, the Athletics broke with another recent tradition and began to allow second baseman Phil Garner to remain in the game rather than pinch hitting for him at the first opportunity as they had so often done with his predecessors. Ted Kubiak, Garner's primary backup, was dispatched to San Diego in exchange for much needed starting pitching help in the presence of veteran Sonny Siebert. A short time later the Athletics were able to convince the Cleveland Indians to part with veteran starters Jim Perry and Dick Bosman in exchange for Blue Moon Odom. It was the end of an eleven-year stint in an Athletic uniform for Odom, and his contributions as a starting pitcher, pinch runner, and clubhouse presence were essential to the past successes of the ballclub. While the thirty-one year-old Bosman, the thirty-eight year-old Siebert, and thirty-nine year-old Perry cut a much more mature profile than the youthful Athletic pitching staffs of the past, their veteran presence did serve to take up part of the strain on Holtzman and Blue. The Athletics added another experienced starter in a deal just prior to the June 15 trading deadline, acquiring Stan Bahnsen from the fading White Sox in exchange for Dave Hamilton. Bahnsen was a former twenty game winner who had run afoul of White Sox management due to a contract dispute.

The Athletics won thirteen out of fourteen games after completing the Bahnsen deal, giving them a comfortable seven and a half game lead over Kansas City at the end of June. Despite the evolution of the Kansas City Royals, the Athletics' grip on the top spot was never really challenged as the season progressed. The Athletics held with their tradition of padding their roster with a cadre of experienced supporting players in late season waiver deals, securing the services of the versatile Cesar Tovar and Tommy Harper, in addition to the reactivation of coach Dal Maxvill. It would be the reliable and patient Maxvill's third and final stint with the Athletics. The season ended on a strange note, with Alvin Dark foregoing the use of a designated hitter in the next-to-last game of the season.

Despite the challenges of replacing Hunter and the fact that Claudell Washington was the only regular to hit above .280, the Athletics were never seriously challenged as divisional leaders. Their fifth straight divisional title came as easily as any they had won previously, and their

Hollow Victory

.605 winning percentage reversed three consecutive seasons of declining performance in that category. There was great cause for optimism as the team prepared to compete for their fourth straight League Championship.

The Athletics' opponents in their fifth straight League Championship Series would be the Red Sox of Boston. The Red Sox had enjoyed an amazing season, defeating the heavily favored Baltimore Orioles and New York Yankees to unexpectedly win their division. The failure of the Yankees was a particular surprise. The team had finished just two games behind the Orioles the previous season, and their off season acquisition of Catfish Hunter and Bobby Bonds made them the consensus choice to win the 1975 championship. Hunter delivered twenty-three wins for his new club, but it was not enough to launch the Yankees to the top. The Red Sox rocketed from nowhere, largely on the contribution of rookie sensations Fred Lynn and Jim Rice. The Red Sox featured a balanced offensive attack supported by a solid pitching staff that positioned them as the most formidable playoff opponent the Athletics had faced since the disastrous 1971 series. Heightening this challenge was the Athletics' dependence upon lefty starters Holtzman and Blue in the face of an intimidating array of right handed hitters in the Red Sox lineup, a situation exacerbated by the opening of the series at Fenway Park, as dangerous a place for left-handed pitchers as there has ever been.

Rise and Fall

From the very beginning the series was a disaster for the Athletics. The Athletics, whose post-season composure was supposed to be their strong suit, began by making three errors in the first inning of game one. They would go on to allow five unearned runs in a 7-1 loss. While the defense melted down, the offense was stymied by Red Sox ace Luis Tiant, who held the Athletics to only three hits.

The 1975 playoffs featured the long-awaited post-season debut of Billy Williams. The future Hall of Famer had spent his entire major league career with the lowly Chicago Cubs and had never showcased his talents in post-season play. Although his 1975 batting average was a career low .244, he had driven in eighty-one runs and was a very effective designated hitter. He had also hit left handed pitching very effectively throughout his career. Yet Dark chose to pinch hit for Williams with weak hitting Don Hopkins in game one and then to bench Williams in game two against Boston lefty Roger Moret, opting to start .140 hitter Ray Fosse. After waiting sixteen years for a chance to perform in the post-season, Williams ended the League Championship Series with a meager 0-7 performance at the plate.

Despite the odd lineup choice, the Athletics' fortunes seemed to be reversing when a two run, first inning home run by Reggie Jackson gave them a quick 2-0 lead in game two. The lead was expanded to 3-0 before disaster struck in the Red Sox half of the fourth. The Sox greeted Athletic starter Vida Blue with four straight hits and Dark foolishly lifted his ace in favor of Jim Todd with the score tied 3-3 and six innings still left to play. When Todd gave up an inning opening double in the bottom

Hollow Victory

of the fifth, Dark brought in Rollie Fingers. The normally dependable Fingers yielded runs in the sixth, seventh, and eighth innings, resulting in a 6-3 Athletic loss.

With no margin for error, the Athletics returned to Oakland for game three with the hope that the change of venue would also change the dynamics of the series. Not trusting Sonny Siebert, Dick Bosman, or Stan Bahnsen with the start in the do-or-die game, Dark chose to rely on Ken Holtzman, who would be appearing on just two days rest. It was a fateful decision. Claudell Washington's second error of the short series resulted in a Boston run in the third inning. Holtzman was knocked from the hill an inning later as the Red Sox rallied for three more runs. The Athletics closed the score to 5-3 with a two-run rally in the bottom of the eighth, but it was too little, too late; the Red Sox held on to win and secure a shocking three game sweep of the defending champions. Bert Campaneris (0-11), Billy North (0-10), Billy Williams (0-7), and Gene Tenace (0-9) all went hitless, and the lack of starting pitching depth was a death knell for the team.

For the first time in four years, the Athletics watched the World Series on television. The good news was that their lineup was still essentially intact, and despite the disappointing performance in the playoffs it was still a formidable force. The Kansas City Royals were growing stronger, and if the Athletics were going to extend their divisional title streak to six in 1976 they would need to build up their starting pitching. Compounding matters were Vida Blue's notorious moodiness and questions regarding Ken Holtzman's commitment to the game. But good pitching was at a premium, and the Athletics' minor league system was not producing young, quality starters like it had a decade earlier.

Alvin Dark and Charlie Finley were the ultimate baseball odd couple. Despite their differences, Dark dutifully obeyed Finley's every whim, prompting famed New York Daily News cartoonist Bill Gallo to depict Dark as a marionette whose strings were pulled by master puppeteer Finley. The club's untimely post-season exit, coming on the heels of the pressure cooker world of managing for Charlie Finley, fueled speculation that Dark would resign as manager of the Athletics if he was not fired by Finley first. But Dark was eager to return to his job. And he may have had the opportunity to do so, had it not been for a public comment made by Dark to a group of Christian friends after the League Championship Series. To illustrate a story from Christian scripture, Dark used Finley as an example. His exact words are the subject of some dispute, but it was reported that Dark stated that Finley would be "going to hell if he did not change his ways". Finley's reaction was predictable – he fired Dark, claiming that his "outside activities" (a thinly veiled reference to Dark's Christian activism) were too much of a distraction. Finley had fired many managers, but even for him this was a strange way to end a managerial term. Strange or not, the Oakland Athletics would have a new manager to guide them through the challenges ahead. Little

Hollow Victory

did Finley or anyone else know just how daunting those challenges would turn out to be.

The Fall

The Beginning of the End

The first objective of the Athletics after their early exit from the 1975 post-season was to find a new field manager. While the prospect of working for Charlie Finley, with his proclivity for systematically harassing and then firing managers, was certainly less than appealing, the idea of managing the team that had won five consecutive divisional titles was undoubtedly attractive for top-tier managerial candidates. Finley reportedly wanted the volatile Gene Mauch, recently fired by the Montreal Expos for whom he had been the manager for all of their seven major league seasons, but the two were unable to reach an agreement and Mauch accepted the position as manager of the Minnesota Twins.

Chuck Tanner had managed the Chicago White Sox from the waning days of the 1970 season until the day he was fired after a disappointing 1975 campaign. Along the way Tanner had won one Manager of the Year award and had transformed a dismal White Sox team into one of the major challengers to the supremacy of the Oakland Athletics. But Sox management had grown impatient with their continuing status as also-rans, and Tanner, originally a "player's manager" known for maintaining a close relationship with his ballplayers, was beginning to suffer from the effect of deep dissention in the clubhouse. Out of such material, Charlie Finley often found appealing managerial candidates. Chuck Tanner was hired as the man to extend the Athletics' domination of the western division. But before Tanner could take the reigns of the club, the baseball world would be rocked to its core by the McNally / Messersmith decision and the advent of the free agent era in Major League Baseball.

Free agency presented a particular problem for Charlie Finley. Finley was not financially positioned to compete with a growing pool of very wealthy owners for free agent talent. Many of these owners were in a position very similar to Finley's when he originally bought the Athletics. These were powerful men, armed with significant financial resources and hungry for the prestige that would come with owning a championship team. Despite enjoying a string of championships, Finley was unable to translate success on the field to success on the general ledger. In addition, Finley had spent the last several years burning virtually every bridge that had formerly existed with his players. Some of the animosity dated back to some of Finley's old habits of harassing his employees. Finley believed that all of his employees, including his field personnel, were simply hired hands, subject to whatever treatment Finley chose to dole out. Finley could exhibit unbridled generosity to a player one minute, then act like a penny-pinching miser with that same player the very next. For example, Finley generously lent players money, then called the loan and garnished their wages immediately afterward if his own financial situation dictated it. Chief among the dividing points between Finley and his players was the relatively new process of salary arbitration. Baseball players are notoriously sensitive about their bosses publicly criticizing their performance, a key element of any salary arbitration hearing. And owners, used to having their own

The Beginning of the End

way during decades of one-way salary negotiations, would always resent players that won their arbitration cases, often trading them or finding other ways to punish the player. Nowhere was the atmosphere resulting from salary arbitration more poisonous than in Oakland. Because of his hardball negotiating style and lowball salary offers, Finley was subjected to a string of arbitration cases by his star players, with Finley often coming out on the losing side. Finley's bitterness toward the victorious players was compounded by the negative impact that it had on his financial bottom line. In any event, Finley's roster was chock full of angry, bitter players eager to flee Finley. Players that would be welcomed with open arms and open checkbooks by other major league owners as eager to strip Finley of his talent as they were to further their own championship dreams.

With the new Basic Agreement negotiated, signed, and in place for the beginning of the 1976 season, the members of the Oakland Athletics not covered by existing multi-year contracts wasted no time in declaring that they were playing out their option year in preparation for entering the free agent market at the conclusion of the season. Joe Rudi, Rollie Fingers, Gene Tenace, Bert Campaneris, Sal Bando, Reggie Jackson, and Ken Holtzman all set in motion the process that would eventually end their relationship with Finley and the Athletics. With the exception of Holtzman, all of those players had been with Finley through their entire careers. Unless something dramatic happened to forestall the inevitable, Charlie Finley would be without seven of his star players when 1977 began. Finley understood as well as anyone the price that these players would bring on the open market, and he could have signed the majority of them for far less than market value had he chosen to do so. Instead, Finley bargained as if the free agent process did not exist. His initial salary offers demonstrated either immense stubbornness or a complete denial of reality or both. Many of the stars responsible for Finley's success right through the 1975 season were offered tiny raises or no raises at all; Bando was actually offered a 20% salary *decrease*. Finley's approach to negotiating with his players virtually guaranteed their departure following the season.

Suddenly, the loss of Catfish Hunter did not seem like such a catastrophic blow after all. Instead of trying to replace a single player, Finley was now faced with the prospect of losing virtually the entire core of his team.

Break Up the A's

It is one of the great paradoxes in baseball history. Despite the incredible turmoil caused by the owner, one of the keys to the A's domination during the 1970's was the stability of their roster. After building the foundation in the 1960's and early 1970's, Charlie Finley fielded a lineup that was remarkably stable from 1971-1975, fine tuning whenever necessary but maintaining the core personnel intact. With the lone exception of the loss of Catfish Hunter following the 1974 season, the team seemed to grow stronger with each successive year. But that was about to change.

The Athletics stood pat during the off season following their loss to the Red Sox in the 1975 League Championship Series. Perhaps distracted by the free agency and Alvin Dark soap operas, and despite the clear need for a strong right-handed starting pitcher, the only roster moves of significance were the releases of veteran players Sonny Siebert and Tommy Harper and the sale of Ray Fosse to the Cleveland Indians. But this was truly the calm before the storm.

The situation between Charlie Finley and Reggie Jackson had gone from bad to worse with the advent of free agency. Once again Jackson was unhappy with Finley's 1976 contract offer, and he made no secret that his goal was free agency and a big payday at the end of the season. For his part, Finley recognized that one of his most valuable

Rise and Fall

assets was about to be stripped from him with virtually no compensation. The wheels were therefore set in motion for a series of events that would land Charlie Finley right back into a confrontation with Major League Baseball Commissioner Bowie Kuhn.

Under new manager Chuck Tanner, the 1976 version of the Athletics still appeared ready to step up to the challenge of winning their sixth straight divisional title when the spring training camps finally opened after the new Basic Agreement was negotiated. The team still boasted one the strongest lineups in the game, as well as some of the top pitchers. Within their division, the Kansas City Royals were viewed as the defending champion's greatest threat, but the Royals did not have a power hitter to compare with the likes of Reggie Jackson and they lacked dominant pitchers like Vida Blue and Rollie Fingers. Despite the fact that the winter trading season had not brought an influx of significant new talent, Tanner still had an impressive lineup with which to compete. One noteworthy addition to the roster was backup infielder Larry Lintz, acquired from the St. Louis Cardinals in a minor trade after the 1975 playoffs. Lintz was the heir to the pinch running specialist role previously held by Allen Lewis, Herb Washington, and Don Hopkins. In contrast to his predecessors, Lintz was a complete player who was also one of the National League's top base stealers, stealing as many as 50 bases during his brief career in the senior circuit. From the beginning of Tanner's reign with the ballclub it was apparent that the Athletics would be off to the races, relying on Billy North, Bert Campaneris, Phil Garner,

Break Up the A's

Claudell Washington and Lintz to drive the opposition crazy with their constant base stealing. All appeared to be well as spring training drew to a close. Nobody was prepared for the bombshell that was about to explode.

On April 2, just one week before the opening of the regular season, the Oakland Athletics shocked the baseball world by trading Reggie Jackson.

The prospect of Jackson's looming free agency, coupled with the increasing friction between Jackson and Finley, drove the Athletics' owner to part with the superstar that had played his entire career with the Athletic organization. In addition to Jackson, Finley also included star lefthander Ken Holtzman in a trade with the Baltimore Orioles that brought the Athletics a package that included young slugger Don Baylor and right handed starting pitchers Mike Torrez and Paul Mitchell. Like Jackson, Holtzman was also eligible for free agency and had also worn out his welcome with Finley. Jackson was devastated by the deal. He refused to report to the Orioles, a situation that grew worse when they automatically renewed his contract with a forced pay cut. By the time Jackson negotiated an agreement to report to the Orioles, he had missed the entire month of April. In any event, Reggie Jackson was no longer Charlie Finley's problem.

In Jackson's absence the Athletics got off to a lackluster start. By mid-May the team was playing .500 baseball and wallowing in fourth

Rise and Fall

place. The team then suffered through an eight-game losing streak that left the club with their worst mid-season record since the darkest days of 1967. Matters improved marginally, but as the June 15 trading deadline approached they were still well below the .500 mark, in fifth place, ten and a half games behind the division-leading Royals. The season was slipping away and everyone waited for Finley to make a move to shake things up. Finley did make his move, but it was not the move anyone expected.

On June 15, Charlie Finley threw in the towel on the 1976 season, despite the fact that there were still over one hundred games to play. With the trading deadline upon him, his championship team in fifth place, eleven games out of first place, and the probable defection of his top stars to free agency, Finley began to disband his team. Taking a page from his predecessor, Connie Mack, Finley chose to simultaneously cut his losses and acquire much-needed cash by selling his top stars. On June 15, Finley sold Vida Blue to the New York Yankees for $1.5 million and Rollie Fingers and Joe Rudi to the Boston Red Sox for $2 million. The defending champion Red Sox were at that time trailing the division-leading Yankees by six games, and both teams were elated to acquire seasoned stars like Blue, Rudi, and Fingers. Each team felt that their deal was exactly what they needed to win the division. The Athletics and their fans, still shocked by the April trade of Reggie Jackson, saw this as the death knell for their team. Any hope that the team would recover and bring home another title had all but faded. But in a season filled with the unexpected, nobody could have predicted the events that would occur.

Break Up the A's

Baseball Commissioners traditionally wield almost absolute power in the sport. In addition to enforcing the written rules, Commissioners often apply liberal interpretations to vague principles that outline their general duties. One of the duties of the Commissioner is to ensure that the integrity of the game remains unquestioned. This responsibility has resulted in Commissioners inserting themselves into situations in which the written rules fall short of guaranteeing the interest of the sport. As an example, Commissioner Bowie Kuhn intervened during the 1972 holdout of Vida Blue, an action not supported by any rules or precedent; in Kuhn's opinion, the absence of Blue was economically damaging to all of the teams in the league and he considered it in the "best interests of baseball" to intervene and broker a settlement. In the case of Blue, Rudi, and Fingers, Kuhn was concerned that a purely cash transaction for stars of the caliber of those three players set a precedent by which wealthy teams could simply use their financial strength to purchase players while teams without equivalent financial resources would be left at a disadvantage. Although there was logic to Kuhn's argument, the history of baseball was replete with examples of wealthy owners using their assets to build up their teams. The Yankees purchased Babe Ruth in 1920 for $100,000 in a cash-only deal. In the days prior to the amateur draft, wealthy owners paid as much as $205,000 for players that had never even worn a major league uniform. A little more than a year earlier, the Yankees paid over $3 million to sign Catfish Hunter. Nevertheless, Kuhn decided that the sale of players for such large cash amounts was not in the best interest of baseball in that it tipped the competitive balance of the game unfairly toward wealthy teams. Kuhn's decision, another in a string of calls by

Rise and Fall

the Commissioner that went against the Athletics, prompted Finley to call the Commissioner "the village idiot", a statement unlikely to endear the owner to the game's top executive. This time Finley had allies, as Kuhn's decision also drew the ire of Yankees owner George Steinbrenner and Red Sox owner Tom Yawkey. The protests of the impacted owners notwithstanding, Blue, Rudi, and Fingers were still Oakland Athletics. The matter grew even more complicated as Finley initially refused to accept Kuhn's decision. Considering the three players to be the property of their new teams, Finley refused to allow them to suit up while he escalated the matter through the courts. Kuhn in turn refused to allow the Athletics to replace the players on the roster, forcing the Athletics to compete with just twenty-two players on their roster for two weeks in the second half of June. But the Commissioner is the ultimate authority in baseball, and Finley had to eventually concede defeat – Blue, Rudi, and Fingers eventually rejoined the Athletics and the sales were officially and permanently cancelled. Finley would attempt to move Blue twice more in future years, with trades to the Rangers in 1977 and to the Reds in 1978 both nullified by Kuhn.

The Athletics continued to struggle as the summer wore on, but by early August they had risen as high as second place, although they were still barely above .500 and were twelve games behind the front-running Kansas City Royals. But the Athletics were not finished yet. Chuck Tanner's club suddenly came alive, reeling off a nine-game winning streak to cut the Royals lead to seven games in mid-August. The fuel that drove the Athletics' offensive engine in the absence of Reggie Jackson was the stolen base. Under Tanner, the Athletics were on their way to setting an American League record with a total of 341 stolen bases. Phil Garner, Bert Campaneris, Billy North, Claudell Washington, Don Baylor, and Larry Lintz each stole over thirty bases, with North leading the way with seventy-five. North seemed reinvigorated by the departure of Jackson, a long-standing antagonist of the center fielder. Finley and Tanner added a second pinch running specialist, Matt Alexander, who stole twenty bases. Even Sal Bando got into the act, adding a career-high twenty steals. As he did so effectively throughout the Athletics championship streak, Finley used the waiver process to bolster his lineup for the stretch drive against the Royals, acquiring veterans Nate Colbert, Willie McCovey, and Ron Fairly. The lack of depth in the starting rotation proved to be the largest impediment to the A's comeback, and without big winners like Hunter and Holtzman on the pitching staff, the Athletics were unable to put together an extended hot streak. Fortunately for the Athletics, the Royals slowly self-destructed during the month of September and the Athletics slowly ate away at their lead. But the Royals eventually ran out the clock, and when the season ended the Athletics found themselves in second place for the first time since 1970, a mere two and a half games behind the Royals.

The Athletic players publicly blasted Finley for costing the team their sixth straight divisional championship by disrupting the team with the attempted sale of Blue, Rudi, and Fingers. The Athletics believed that the loss of their three stars for the two-week, mid-season period cost them the divisional title. While we will never know how things would have ended had Finley not attempted the sale or if he had reinstated the

Rise and Fall

players immediately upon Kuhn's intercession, the club was 7-5 during the period in which the three stars were in limbo. What is clear is that the Athletics just weren't good enough to catch the Royals, and one of the great championship streaks in sports was now over. For the first time since 1970, the Athletics would be out of the post-season. It would be five years before the team would return to post-season play, and twelve years before they would return to the World Series.

In the meantime, the Oakland Athletics were about to suffer one of the greatest falls of any team in the history of baseball.

Exodus

The fate of the Oakland Athletics was sealed on November 1, 1976. On that day, Sal Bando, Don Baylor, Bert Campaneris, Rollie Fingers, Joe Rudi, and Gene Tenace joined former Athletic Reggie Jackson as the first class of free agents, as did the recently acquired Nate Colbert and Willie McCovey. Per the terms of the newly minted agreement between the owners and the Players Association, free agents would be subject to a new "re-entry draft" in which teams would vie for the right to negotiate with the available players. This was a small concession to the owners, who thought that any chance to mitigate the size of the newly defined open market would contribute in at least a small way toward keeping salary growth in check. Any doubts about the implications of free agency on player salaries quickly evaporated when the Boston Red Sox signed relief pitcher Bill Campbell two days after the draft. Campbell, with four solid but unremarkable seasons of pitching in relative obscurity for the lowly Minnesota Twins under his belt, scored a $1,000,000 deal, a significant increase for a player that had earned $23,000 the previous season. In the feeding frenzy that followed, it was Reggie Jackson who was considered the jewel of the free agent pack. All of baseball waited to see what Jackson's value would be on the open market. Not surprising, Jackson scored a huge payday with a package totaling $3,000,000 courtesy of the New York Yankees. With big money like that being handed out, any chance of Charlie Finley retaining his free agent stars faded from very slim to zero.

Rise and Fall

The Athletics participated in the inaugural re-entry draft, claiming the rights to negotiate with many of their departing stars as well as many of the other marquee players available. In the end, the Athletics were unable to sign any of the players for whom they had negotiation rights acquired through the re-entry draft. The only victory achieved in the first cycle of modern free agency came outside of the mainstream free agent process. The nomadic Dick Allen earned free agency after the re-entry process was finalized, necessitating a special re-entry draft in which Allen was the only player eligible. The Oakland Athletics were the only team to select him. Allen held out until the following spring before agreeing to become Oakland's first free agent acquisition, a small compensation for the loss of so many great stars.

Adding insult to injury, the team lost pitcher Glenn Abbott and two other players in an expansion draft a few days later. Manager Chuck Tanner also departed. In a move reminiscent of the Dick Williams fiasco, Finley negotiated a deal in which the Pittsburgh Pirates were allowed to sign Tanner as their manager – in return the Pirates shipped veteran catcher Manny Sanguillen to the Athletics. The disappointing Billy Williams was released in November of 1976. The following March, Finley traded Phil Garner to the Pirates and Claudell Washington to the Texas Rangers. With the departure of Garner and Washington, every impact player from the Athletics' 1975 divisional championship team except for Vida Blue and Billy North had left the ballclub.

Almost lost in the mass exodus was the sale of reliever Paul Linblad to the Texas Rangers for the princely sum of $400,000 in

Exodus

February of 1977. As the move was reminiscent of the controversy surrounding the attempted sale of Blue, Fingers, and Rudi the previous summer, Finley knew that this deal would draw the immediate attention of Commissioner Bowie Kuhn since it flew in the face of Kuhn's clear decree that the sale of players for large sums of cash would not be allowed. Predictably, the Commissioner did step in, temporarily interrupting the transaction. Kuhn eventually concluded that it was the Rangers, not Finley, who initiated the trade; thus the sale was allowed to proceed, further blurring the lines around what transactions were permissible and where the limits for cash deals were set. Bizarre logic was in great supply when it came to the strange Kuhn / Finley relationship.

On March 15, 1978, Charlie Finley finally succeeded in structuring a trade of Vida Blue that met the criteria set down by Bowie Kuhn. Blue's declining fortunes had mirrored that of the Athletics, and he lost a remarkable total of nineteen games in 1977. The former Most Valuable Player and Cy Young Award winner was dealt across the bay to the San Francisco Giants in return for seven players and a reported $300,000 in cash. None of the players made an impact on the Athletics, while Blue would go on to win eighteen games for his new employer in what was to be his last great season. With the departure of Blue, none of the players from Finley's first World Championship remained with the organization just six years after that milestone event. A few weeks later the housecleaning was complete when Billy North was dealt to the Los

Rise and Fall

Angeles Dodgers for a reserve outfielder. North was eligible for free agency at the end of the season, and Finley did not want to repeat the experience of losing a top player with little tangible compensation.

One of the greatest dynasties in the history of sports had been dismantled virtually overnight. It had taken Finley ten years to build the club from a baseman dweller to a first place team – it took only two to dismantle it. Free agency, greed, avarice, stinginess, and petty grudges had done what the competition could not do – stop the Athletics.

After the Storm

Jack McKeon was the man given the unenviable task of managing the post free agency Oakland Athletics into the 1977 season. For the first time since the 1960's, the Athletics' opening day lineup was missing the likes of Bando, Campaneris, Rudi, and Tenace. Backing up Billy North in their place was a strange hodgepodge that included veteran journeymen such as Dick Allen, Earl Williams, Marty Perez, and Manny Sanguillen and untried youngsters Rob Picciolo, Wayne Gross, Mitchell Page, and Tony Armas. Even Billy Conigliaro, who had not played a major league game since leaving the Athletics in 1973, was given a spring tryout. The pitching staff featured a few decent, established starters of the likes of Vida Blue, Mike Torrez, George Medich, and Stan Bahnsen, supported by youngsters Rick Langford and Mike Norris. But the bullpen and the bench were terribly thin, and this roster was a patchwork quilt, hastily pieced together to field a team in the face of the most dramatic and permanent drain of skilled personnel any professional baseball team had ever faced.

Under the dire circumstances facing the revamped Athletics, few expected the club to be a factor in the 1977 pennant race. It was therefore quite a shock when the team got off to its best start in a franchise history that dated back to 1901, winning seven out of its first eight games. Like their predecessors, the newly minted Oakland Athletics were again at the top of their division.

It was all a mirage.

Rise and Fall

Not long after the blazing start the team started to lose. Not a lot at first. After two months the club was just a game below .500, but the impatient Finley fired McKeon. His replacement was coach Bobby Winkles. Winkles had risen to prominence as the coach of the renowned Arizona State baseball program that had produced, among others, Reggie Jackson, Sal Bando, and Rick Monday. Under Winkles the bottom fell out. The team lost two out of every three games the rest of the way, finishing dead last in the division behind the expansion Seattle Mariners. Although Winkles had the worst record of any Athletic manager since the unfortunate Luke Appling in the latter days of the disastrous 1967 season, Finley brought Winkles back for the 1978 season. Once again the club got off to a roaring start, this time winning nineteen out of its first twenty-four games and opening up a four game first-place lead in early May. Two weeks later, with the team still in first place, manager Winkles walked away, unable to continue to serve as an employee of Charlie Finley. His replacement was Jack McKeon, the very same manager Finley fired almost exactly a year before. The team responded by losing nine of their next twelve games. The team stabilized for a while and played an unexpected role in the race for the divisional title. As late as June 7 the team was ten games over .500 and at the top of the division. The club then suffered a ten game losing streak that served as a taste of things still to come. Undaunted, the Athletics rallied to again regain the divisional lead. The team played reasonably well for the next several weeks, and as late as August 11 they were five games over .500 and still in title contention. The team then proceeded to self-destruct, accumulating a dismal 8-37 record the rest of the way. Without the likes of Bando, Hunter, Jackson, and Rudi to rally the team and stop the slide, the Athletics were doomed. They escaped the cellar, finishing sixth in the seven-team western division. With the pattern of losing now set, the club followed the 1978 meltdown by finishing last in the division in 1979 while losing 108 games, the most by any Athletic team since 1916.

The Athletics' dynasty had clearly come to an end.

The Athletics' players spent the Octobers of 1977 and 1978 in the comfort of their homes, likely watching former Athletics Catfish Hunter and Reggie Jackson lead their new team, the New York Yankees, to two consecutive World Championships. Under the glare of the New York spotlight, Jackson had become a truly national sports hero. His World Series performances with the Yankees also boosted his image as the one of the truly great post-season performers in sports history. In the hands of Jackson, the torch of a dynasty was passed from Oakland to New York. But the emerging Yankee dynasty was built in a manner far differently than that of the Oakland Athletics. True, a small core group of players including Thurman Munson, Roy White, and Ron Guidry had grown up in the Yankee farm system, but they were the exception on a team that had largely been built through trades, player purchases, and most importantly the free agent market. From now on, this is the way baseball dynasties would be built. There would be other great teams and other dynasties to follow, but there would never again be a team like the Oakland Athletics – built from the ground up and held together for an

Rise and Fall

extended period without free agency-inspired turnover. Baseball was about to enter a totally new era.

For Sale

With his ballclub in tatters, his financial coffers and his ballpark seats empty, and no prospects, Charlie Finley's options for turning around the Athletics were very limited. Unable to compete in the new landscape, Finley sought to revive his organization's fortunes by relocating the club. Finley attempted to move the franchise to Denver and later to New Orleans. All attempts to move the club or sell them to buyers that wanted to move it were thwarted by the city of Oakland. Under the terms of the team's lease with the city, the Athletics would be making Oakland their home for the next decade. The final straw came when Finley's divorce from his wife Shirley was finally settled. Finley's operation of the Athletics had been hamstrung for years by issues with his wife, who was also his business partner. Finley attempted to negotiate a deal with his estranged wife that would give her ongoing equity in the ballclub, but like the owner's absent superstars, Shirley Finley wanted a clean break from Finley. At the same time, the ill health that had plagued Finley throughout his adult life once again debilitated him. Between his medical and financial situation, Finley's days as the Athletics' owner were numbered.

Finley's personal crises could not have come at a worse time. Finley hired fireball maverick Billy Martin to manage the wallowing ballclub for the 1980 season. Martin was the perfect manager for the struggling Athletics. Branding his aggressive style of play "Billyball" during his first season at the helm of the Athletics, Martin drew the very best out of each and every player on the roster. The club became an overnight sensation, once again serving as a force within the western division while generating fan enthusiasm unknown even during the heyday of the championship years. With the club rising in the standings and the turnstiles churning, it should have been a period of celebration for Finley as his Athletics rose from the ashes. But it was not to be. Finley's sole remaining option was to put his prized possession, his baseball team, up for sale.

On August 23, 1980 Charles O. Finley completed the sale of his beloved Athletics to Walter Haas, owner of Levi-Strauss, for $12.7 million. The sale price was over $5 million less than the total 1977 free agent contract packages for Catfish Hunter, Joe Rudi, Rollie Fingers, Gene Tenace, Bert Campaneris, Sal Bando, Don Baylor, Reggie Jackson, and Ken Holtzman.

Charlie Finley lived for another sixteen years after selling the Athletics. His health and financial resources steadily declined during his final years until he had all but completely lost both. Finley died on February 19, 1996, just days before his seventy-eighth birthday. His former players were gracious when news of his death reached them, with several, including former adversaries Catfish Hunter and Reggie Jackson, commenting about Finley's dedication to excellence and his pioneering approach to modernizing the game of baseball. But the praise for the former owner was largely suppressed. Finley went to his grave having

For Sale

left many enemies in his wake. He also left an indelible mark on the game of baseball, both on the field and in the ledger books. His impact will be felt for generations. Perhaps one day his feat of assembling one of the sport's greatest teams will receive the recognition it is due. With the passing of generations and the ebb of bad feelings Finley aroused, the likelihood that the maverick will one day earn a place on the baseball Hall of Fame will rightfully increase.

What If?

It is certainly pure conjecture, but it is interesting to consider how the fortunes of the Athletics might have fared had the free agencies of Hunter, McNally, and Messersmith not occurred. Would the team have continued their domination of the American League western division, and would there have been future post-season glory for the team?

One of the major factors in favor of the Athletics continued domination of their division was the lack of a strong successor at the top of the standings. In a great irony, the "Oakland era" of the history of the American League western division was followed by the "Kansas City era"; the Kansas City Royals ended up flourishing in the very city that Charlie Finley wrote off after the 1967 season. The Royals record within the division was certainly impressive; beginning in 1976, the team began an eleven-year run in which they finished first or second every year. The Royals followed the Athletics' five-year stint as divisional champions by winning the division three consecutive years from 1976-1978. Unfortunately the Royals ran into the New York Yankees, featuring former Athletics Catfish Hunter and Reggie Jackson, in each of the League Championship Series during that period, losing all three series to superior Yankee teams. The Royals had definitely built a winning club, but they did so in the face of a relative lack of strong competition in the division. Had the Athletics maintained the core of their championship teams it is not difficult to imagine that they could have challenged and possibly overcome the Royals.

What If?

It is interesting to consider how the fortunes of the Athletics in the 1975 playoffs would have changed had Charlie Finley honored his contractual commitment to Catfish Hunter and retained his pitching ace. With a balanced pitching rotation featuring the right-handed Hunter, it is possible, although unlikely, that the Athletics could have mounted a stronger defense of their league title against the Red Sox. Even with Hunter, overcoming the awesome Red Sox lineup in a short series would not have been easy, particularly given Hunter's 0-3 record against the Red Sox in 1975 and the anemic performance of the Oakland hitters in the playoffs. Had Finley retained Hunter, Ken Holtzman, and Reggie Jackson through the 1976 season, however, there is a much higher likelihood that the outcome of that pennant race would have been different. Even if they posted sub-par seasons, Hunter and Holtzman would have added significantly to the depth of the Oakland starting rotation. This, coupled with Jackson's offensive contribution, would have probably enabled the Athletics to overtake the Royals. A repeat World Championship would not have been so likely. Even without Hunter, the eastern division champion New York Yankees had a deep pitching staff. And even if the Athletics had succeeded in defeating the Yankees in the playoffs, the National League Champion Cincinnati Reds were a juggernaut likely to smash the Athletics as easily as they had the Yankees in the 1976 World Series. Yet that intangible quality that the Athletics possessed, that ability to win in the face of adversity, may well have tipped the balance in their favor.

From an age perspective, the nucleus of the Athletic roster was still considered to be in their prime in 1977. Despite this, it is arguable that for many of the players who opted to leave the team via free agency, their best playing days were now behind them.

McDonald's Hamburger billionaire Ray Kroc and his San Diego Padres were the winners of the sweepstakes to sign thirty year-old free agents Gene Tenace and Rollie Fingers. For Tenace, the years in San Diego were not productive ones. He spent four years as a solid contributor for the club, but his best days were clearly behind him. The former World Series hero made one last fall classic appearance with the St. Louis Cardinals in 1982, going 0-5 at the plate. A year later he was out of the game. Fingers fared much better with the Padres, becoming one of the top relief pitchers in the National League. Fingers' best days came when he returned to the American League as a member of the Milwaukee Brewers in 1981. With Milwaukee, Fingers solidified his credentials as a future Hall of Famer by matching former teammate Vida Blue's achievement of winning both the American League Most Valuable Player and Cy Young awards in 1981 and later leading the Brewers to the 1982 American League Championship. An arm injury cost Fingers the opportunity to pitch in the 1982 World Series. He retired from the game after the 1985 season at the age of thirty-eight.

Captain Sal Bando chose Milwaukee as his new home after leaving the Athletics. Bando initially maintained his record as a durable, steady contributor, but at the age of thirty-three he was clearly past his prime. Bando's performance steadily declined over the five years he spent in a Brewer uniform, a stint that ended with his retirement in 1981

What If?

at the age of thirty-seven. The former field general of the Athletics moved to the Brewers front office as the club's general manager.

Joe Rudi's free agency home with the California Angels was not a happy one. Age and injuries significantly hampered Rudi's performance, and he was considered one of the bigger disappointments of the initial class of free agents. After four sub-par seasons with the Angels, Rudi found himself traded to the Boston Red Sox, the same team whose purchase of Rudi was voided by Bowie Kuhn in 1976. After a single season with the Red Sox, Rudi again went the free agent route. In a bitter irony, free agent Joe Rudi signed with none other than the Oakland Athletics for his final season in 1982. After leaving the Athletics for the first time after 1976, Joe Rudi never again appeared in a post-season game.

At thirty-four, Bert Campaneris was the veteran of the Athletics' free agent class. Campaneris signed with the Texas Rangers and enjoyed a relatively productive 1977 season. It would be his last year as a regular player. Campaneris faded quickly and was soon dispatched to the California Angels, for whom he made one last post-season appearance as a defensive substitution in 1979. Campaneris ended his career with a single season as a New York Yankee in 1983 before retiring at the age of forty-one.

The New York Yankees benefited the most from Charlie Finley's inability to hold onto his players. Catfish Hunter lived up to his promise by delivering a fifth straight twenty-win season for his new employers in 1975. Although it would be his last season as a twenty-game winner, Hunter would play an essential role in the club's championship seasons from 1976-1978. Suffering from a shoulder injury that likely resulted from pitching an average of 285 innings a year from 1969-1976, Hunter still managed to deliver key victories and provide a steadying influence in the tumultuous Yankee clubhouse during their championship run. Hunter's injury would contribute to his premature retirement from the game after the 1979 season, but not before he had cemented his legacy as one of the greatest pitchers of his generation.

Hunter's pitching partner from the heyday of the Athletics, Ken Holtzman, also joined the Yankees as a result of a trade with the Orioles in 1976. Holtzman forced the Yankees to sign him to a free agent-level contract in 1976. The thirty year-old Holtzman contributed to the Yankee run to the American League Championship in 1976, but then quickly fell into disfavor. He spent then next year and a half in virtual exile in the Yankee bullpen before being shipped to the Chicago Cubs, for whom he pitched until the end of his career in 1979.

Of the entire original free agent group of 1977, none made a bigger splash than Reggie Jackson. Jackson joined former Oakland teammates Hunter and Holtzman as a member of the New York Yankees for the 1977 season. As much as his presence was missed in Oakland, his impact on the Yankees was even more dramatic. Finally playing on a stage big enough to match his massive ego, Jackson delivered. While his time with the Yankees was marred by controversy, the slugging outfielder did lead the club to four post-season appearances in five years,

What If?

including consecutive World Championships in 1977 and 1978. Jackson wore out his welcome in New York and opted again for free agency after the 1981 World Series. Landing with the California Angels, Jackson made two final playoff appearances in 1982 and 1986. It was only fitting that the first superstar of the Oakland Athletics chose to return to play the final season of his career with Oakland in 1987.

Would the Athletics' dynasty have continued were it not for the rulings of Peter Seitz and the alienation of their star players by Charlie Finley? The answer is maybe. While Finley's roster of home-grown talent clearly showed signs of age and decline following their departure from the team, it is not clear what might have been had they remained in Oakland. The Athletics had a cadre of new talent rising through their farm system, including the sensational Rickey Henderson and a group of solid young pitchers. With the core group acting as a bridge to get them through the late 1970's, the team would certainly have presented strong competition for the Royals and may have taken one or more additional divisional titles. As it was, the Athletics enjoyed resurgence when the decade of the eighties arrived. Under new manager Billy Martin, the club returned to its winning ways in 1980 and returned to post-season play with a playoff appearance in 1981. The revamped Athletics closed the eighties by winning three consecutive American League Championships from 1988-1990, returning the World Championship to Oakland in 1989.

As of this writing, it was the only World Championship won by the Athletics in the post-Finley era.

Bibliography

Readers interested in learning more about the teams, players, and other individuals referenced in this book are fortunate in that there has been a robust body of material published by many excellent authors. A sample of these works is listed below.

Allen, Maury (1981). *Mr. October.* Times Books:New York.

Bergman, Ron (1973). *The Mustache Gang.* Dell Publishing:New York.

Dickey, Glenn (2002). *Champions: The Story of the First Two Oakland A's Dynasties – and the Building of the Third.* Triumph Books:Chicago.

Harrelson, Ken & Hirshberg, Al (1969). *Hawk.* Viking Press:New York.

Hunter, Jim "Catfish" & Keteyian, Armen (1989). *Catfish: My Life in Baseball.* Berkley Books:New York.

Kashatus, William C. (1999). *Connie Mack's '29 Triumph: The Rise and Fall of the Philadelphia Athletics Dynasty.* McFarland & Company:Jefferson, NC.

Kelley, Brent (1997). *Baseball's Biggest Blunder: The Bonus Rule of 1953-1957.* Scarecrow Press:Lanham, MD.

Markusen, Bruce (2002). *A Baseball Dynasty: Charlie Finley's Swingin' A's.* St. Johann Press:Haworth, NJ.

Michelson, Herb (1975). *Charlie O.* Bobbs-Merrill Company:Indianapolis, IN.

Peterson, John E. (2003). *The Kansas City Athletics: A Baseball History (1954-1967).* McFarland & Company:Jefferson, NC.

Williams, Dick & Plaschke, Bill (1990). *No More Mr. Nice Guy.* Harcourt Brace Jovanovich:Orlando, FL.

There are also numerous encyclopedias and other reference materials that are valuable sources for detailed information about the subjects contained within this book. Of these, two Internet web sites are particularly convenient sources for statistics, boxscores, and other factual material:

http://retrosheet.org/

http://www.baseball-reference.com/

Index

Abbott, Glenn............223, 226, 248
Aker, Jack 35, 87
Alexander, Doyle 172
Alexander, Matt 245
Allen, Dick................121, 248, 251
Allison, Bob..........................84–85
Alou, Felipe 97–99, 104, 167
Alou, Jesus........................167, 175
Alou, Matty124–25, 127, 129, 132–33, 145, 148, 151, 160, 167
Andersen, Sparky.......145, 148, 153
Andrews, Mike 103, 167, 170, 176–83, 188
Appling, Luke 73–74, 252
Armas, Tony 251
Autry, Gene................................194
Bahnsen, Stan.....121, 228, 231, 251
Bailey, Bob 54
Baker, Frank "Home Run"....10, 13
Bando, Sal....36, 45, 48, 56, 65, 73, 80, 82–83, 87, 90, 95–96, 103, 109, 127, 131, 134, 135–36, 152, 166, 169–70, 186, 194, 201, 207, 221, 226, 237, 245, 247, 251–52, 256, 260
Barry, Jack 10, 13
Bauer, Hank 89, 94, 102
Baylor, Don...... 168, 208, 241, 245, 247, 256
Bench, Johnny........56, 144, 147–53
Bender, Chief....................9–11, 13
Berra, Yogi...................176–78, 181
Billingham, Jack 147, 149, 152
Blasingame, Don.........................64
Blefary, Curt 105, 126
Blue, Vida........36, 44, 96, 100–101, 103–9, 116–18, 122–24, 126, 129–30, 134, 135, 145–46, 149–51, 154, 159, 166–67, 169–71, 176, 199, 207, 210, 223, 226–27, 229–32, 240, 242–45, 248–49, 251, 260
Blyleven, Bert........................... 199
Boggs, Wade 7
Bonds, Bobby 229
Bosman, Dick 227, 231
Boswell, Dave 85
Bourque, Pat 167, 203
Boyer, Clete 26, 34, 125
Brooks, Bobby 114, 121
Brown, Gates 131
Brown, Larry 122
Brown, Ollie 123
Bryan, Billy 35
Buckner, Bill 211–12
Buford, Don 168
Bumbry, Al............................... 170
Buschhorn, Don........................ 48
Campaneris, Bert44–45, 49, 59–61, 64, 67, 80, 82, 87, 90, 95, 96, 127, 133, 132–35, 143, 147–48, 151, 152, 166, 169–70, 175, 182, 209, 211, 231, 237, 240, 245, 247, 251, 256, 261
Campbell, Bill 247
Carbo, Bernie............................ 56
Carew, Rod 201
Carey, Andy............................... 34
Carroll, Clay 149
Carty, Rico............................... 167
Cash, Norm....... 129, 130, 131, 134
Cater, Danny 64, 70, 73, 82, 90, 95, 96
Cepeda, Orlando 123–24, 160, 163, 164
Cerv, Bob 26
Cey, Ron...................................... 2
Chaney, Darrel........................ 153
Charles, Ed 64, 73
Chavarria, Ossie 35

Index

Chilcott, Steve 57
Clemente, Roberto 51
Cochrane, Mickey 23
Colavito, Rocky 41, 59
Colbert, Nate 245, 247
Coleman, Joe 56, 133
Collins, Eddie 10, 13
Concepcion, Dave 144, 151
Conigliaro, Billy .. 56, 162–63, 165, 251
Conigliaro, Tony 72, 162
Coombs, Jack 9–10
Crawford, Willie . 2, 45–46, 54, 211
Cronin, Joe 193
Cuellar, Mike 110, 168, 170, 207
Cullen, Tim 119, 127, 130
Dark, Alvin .. 63, 65, 67, 70–74, 89, 98, 102, 194–95, 198–203, 207, 209, 224, 228, 230–32, 239
Davalillo, Vic ... 167, 169, 175, 188
Davis, Tommy 45, 99, 104, 163, 168
DeMaestri, Joe 26
DiMaggio, Joe 81
Dobson, Chuck 65, 81, 91, 95, 101, 104–9, 110, 113, 119
Donaldson, John 28, 45, 80
Downing, Al 97–99
Duncan, Dave 36, 44, 48, 74, 80, 90, 95, 101, 103, 106, 109, 130, 151–52, 161
Duren, Ryne 26
Durocher, Leo 113
Dyer, Duffy 57
Epstein, Mike 105–6, 124, 131, 134–35, 147, 152, 160
Ermer, Cal 86
Etchebarren, Andy 171
Fairly, Ron 245
Ferguson, Joe 210
Fernandez, Frank 97, 101, 105
Fingers, Rollie 2, 28, 36, 87, 91, 96–97, 103–4, 111, 127, 131, 134, 146–51, 153, 171, 175,

177, 181, 186, 200, 207–10, 211–14, 226, 231, 237, 240, 242–45, 247, 249, 256, 260
Finley, Charlie...24, 28–33, 34, 36–37, 38–42, 43–49, 53–63, 65, 68–74, 75–79, 81–82, 86, 89, 94, 97–102, 103–4, 108–11, 113, 117–19, 122–23, 127, 136, 153, 154–55, 156, 159–64, 167, 174, 178–84, 185–86, 187–95, 196–98, 201, 211, 214, 216–21, 222–24, 225, 227, 233, 235–38, 239–46, 247–50, 252, 259, 261–63, 261–63
Finley, Shirley 255
Fisk, Carlton 56
Fosse, Ray 56, 161–62, 169, 177, 182, 196, 202, 203, 207, 213, 224–26, 230, 239
Foster, George 144
Foxx, Jimmie 23
Francona, Tito 92–94
Freehan, Bill 134, 135
Fregosi, Jim 60
Frick, Ford 30
Fryman, Woody 132
Gallo, Bill 232
Garner, Phil 224–25, 227, 240, 245, 248
Garrett, Wayne 176
Garvey, Steve 209–11
Gentile, Jim 41, 62, 70
Geronimo, Cesar 144, 147, 148
Giambi, Jason 7
Gordon, Joe 32
Gosger, Jim 88
Grant, Jim "Mudcat" 97, 99, 101, 107
Green, Dick ..28, 35–36, 44, 49, 61, 64, 67, 80, 90, 95, 96, 99, 103, 121, 125, 130, 132, 160, 165–66, 178, 196, 203, 211–14, 224
Grich, Bobby 168, 171
Grimsley, Ross 207

267

Gross, Wayne 251
Grote, Jerry 57
Grove, Lefty 23
Guidry, Ron 253
Gullett, Don 149
Haas, Walter 256
Hague, Joe 153
Hamilton, Dave .. 58, 124, 134, 152, 199, 223, 226–27
Haney, Larry 28, 126, 203
Hargan, Steve 198
Harper, Tommy 228, 239
Harrelson, Bud 177
Harrelson, Ken 70–74, 219
Hegan, Mike 105, 131, 147
Heideman, Jack 186
Henderson, Rickey 263
Hendrick, George 114, 132, 135, 145, 148, 151, 161
Hernandez, Jackie 86
Hershberger, Mike 59
Hodges, Gil 192
Holtzman, Ken 56, 113–14, 120, 124, 127, 129, 149, 153, 160, 166, 170, 175, 181, 183, 186, 199–200, 207, 209, 212, 223, 226, 228, 229–32, 237, 241, 245, 256, 259, 262
Hopkins, Don 227, 230, 240
Horlen, Joel 119, 134, 152
Horton, Willie 131
Hoscheit, Vern 201
Houck, Byron 13
Houk, Ralph 189–93
Houston Astros 62
Howard, Frank 95
Howser, Dick 34, 43
Hunter, Jim "Catfish" 28, 36, 45–48, 54, 62, 64, 65, 73, 80–81, 83–87, 90–91, 96, 100–101, 103, 105–10, 113, 120, 124, 127, 129–30, 134, 146, 150, 152, 166, 169, 172, 180–82, 199, 201, 206–7, 210–11, 215, 216–21, 222–24, 228, 229, 238, 239, 243–45, 252–53, 256, 258–59, 261–62
Jackson, Reggie . 28, 36, 45, 57–58, 73, 80, 82, 87, 90, 94–95, 96–98, 103, 106–8, 111, 117–19, 125, 127, 129, 132, 135, 144–45, 147, 154, 166, 178, 182–84, 185–86, 196, 202, 206–10, 224, 226, 230, 237, 239–42, 244, 247, 252–53, 256, 258, 262
Javier, Julian 147
Johnson, Arnold 16, 24–27, 38
Johnson, Bob 92–94
Johnson, Dave 168
Johnson, Deron .. 164–66, 177, 182, 188, 196, 203, 225
Johnstone, Jay 165
Jones, Cleon 176
Joshua, Von 2
Kaline, Al 129, 131
Kaufman, Ewing 19
Keane, Johnny 189
Kelly, Pat 100
Kennedy, Bob 74, 80, 84, 86, 89
Keough, Joe 56, 87
Keough, Marty 56
Killebrew, Harmon . 84–85, 95, 101
Kiner, Ralph 53
Knowles, Darold 105, 129, 175, 186, 200, 225
Koosman, Jerry 175, 182
Koufax, Sandy 91, 113
Krausse, Lew 28, 39, 54, 62, 65, 67–69, 73, 81, 97–98, 162, 179
Kroc, Ray 260
Kubiak, Ted ... 74, 124–25, 130–31, 151, 165, 176, 178, 186, 196, 203, 226, 227
Kuhn, Bowie 122, 143, 179–80, 188, 217–19, 240, 243–45, 249, 261
Lachemann, Marcel 45
Lachemann, Rene 45, 48

Index

Lagrow, Lerrin 132–33
Lajoie, Napoleon 13
Landis, Bill 45
Landis, Jim 59, 62
Lane, Frank 38–39, 43
Langford, Rick 251
LaRussa, Tony 45
Lewis, Allen 150, 152, 170, 196, 240
Linblad, Paul.. 45, 65, 91, 105, 160, 248–49
Lintz, Larry 240, 245
Locker, Bob 134, 160, 196, 225
Lockwood, Skip 48, 54, 62, 88
Lolich, Mickey 130–31, 133
Look, Bruce 86
Lopez, Hector 26, 34
Lumpe, Jerry 34, 43
Lynn, Fred 229
Mack, Connie 9–15, 23–24, 30, 96, 175, 242
    Mack Family.. 16, 24–25, 27, 28
MacPhail, Lee 217
Mangual, Angel ... 45, 99, 105, 109, 114, 121, 130, 145, 150, 151–52, 165, 169, 203, 204
Maris, Roger 26, 34, 95
Marquez, Gonzolo .. 132, 150, 163–67
Marshall, Make 213–14
Marshall, Mike 210
Martin, Billy . 91, 131–33, 255, 263
Matlack, Jon 175
Mauch, Gene 235
Maxvill, Dal... 28, 124–27, 130–31, 133, 134, 165, 228
Mays, Willie 123, 176
McAuliffe, Dick 133
McCovey, Willie 123, 245, 247
McGaha, Mel 61
McGraw, John 10
McGraw, Tug 176–77, 180–81
McGregor, Scott 191, 193
McInnis, Stuffy 10, 13

McKeon, Jack 251–52
McLain, Denny ... 114, 120–21, 124
McNally, Dave 17–18, 109, 168–69, 218, 236, 258
McNamara, John 35, 94, 98, 101
McRae, Hal 144, 147
Medich, George 251
Menke, Dennis ... 144, 146, 149–50, 153
Merritt, Jim 198
Messersmith, Andy 17–18, 56, 218, 236, 258
Millan, Felix 48, 175, 177
Miller, Marvin 115
Milner, John 176–78
Mincher, Don 97, 105, 150
Mitchell, Paul 241
Monday, Rick 36, 45, 55–56, 65, 80, 87, 90, 95–97, 113–14, 160, 252
Monteagudo, Aurelio 45
Morales, Jose 174
Moret, Roger 230
Morgan, Joe . 144, 149, 150–51, 153
Moss, Dick 217
Munson, Thurman 191, 253
Nash, Jim 45, 47, 64–65, 67, 73, 81, 97
Nixon, Richard 122
Nolan, Gary 145, 151
Norman, Freddie 45
Norris, Mike 226, 251
North, Billy 160, 162–63, 166, 169, 175, 196, 202, 211, 231, 240, 245, 248–50, 251
Northrup, Jim 131, 134
O'Brien, Syd 45
O'Donoghue, John 35
O'Riley, Don 88
Odom, John "Blue Moon" 36, 45, 65, 81, 91, 95, 104–5, 110, 113, 119, 121, 124, 127, 129, 131–32, 135–36, 147, 151–53, 171, 199, 206, 208, 223, 226–28

269

Oliva, Tony 84–85
Page, Mitchell 251
Pagliaroni, Jim 80
Palmer, Jim 168–72, 207
Parker, Harry............................ 181
Pena, Orlando............................. 61
Pennock, Herb...................... 11, 13
Perez, Marty............................. 251
Perez, Tony . 144, 146, 148–49, 153
Perry, Gaylord................... 162, 204
Perry, Jim 227
Pettit, Paul................................. 53
Picciolo, Rob............................ 251
Pierce, Tony 45
Pina, Horatio 160, 196
Pizzaro, Juan 93
Plank, Eddie............................ 9–13
Powell, Boog............................ 110
Reese, Rich 86
Reichardt, Rick 45, 54
Reynolds, Tommie................ 45, 59
Rice, Jim 229
Robinson, Frank....................... 168
Robinson, Jackie 146
Rodriguex, Alex........................... 7
Rodriguez, Roberto 45
Rose, Pete ... 144, 150, 152–53, 161
Roseboro, John........................... 86
Rudi, Joe .. 2, 36, 44–45, 48, 62, 67,
  80–81, 95, 97, 101, 103, 127,
  130, 132, 145–46, 167, 170,
  177, 186, 196, 204, 210–11,
  213, 224, 237, 242–45, 247,
  249, 251–53, 256, 261
Ruth, Babe 243
Ryan, Nolan 56, 121
Sanguillen, Manny 248, 251
Scherman, Fred 132
Seaver, Tom 56, 180–82
Seelbach, Chuck....................... 131
Segui, Diego.... 87, 97, 104, 110–11
Seitz, Peter 17–19, 50, 217–18, 263
Shamsky, Art 124
Shawkey, Bob 11, 13

Siebern, Norm 34, 43
Siebert, Sonny 227, 231, 239
Simmons, Al.............................. 23
Sims, Duke 132
Staub, Rusty............................ 176
Steinbrenner, George 7, 31, 190–91,
  193, 244
Stengel, Casey 57, 125, 189
Stone, George 178
Stoneham, Horace 63
Sullivan, Haywood 34, 61–63
Sutton, Don............................. 210
Symington, Stuart.................... 154
Talbot, Fred 59, 61
Tanner, Chuck . 121, 235, 240, 244,
  248
Tartabull, Jose 59
Taylor, Bob "Hawk" 54
Taylor, Brien 58
Tenace, Gene 2, 36, 56, 95, 101,
  106, 126, 130–32, 134–35, 145–
  52, 161, 176, 177, 182, 186,
  203, 224, 231, 237, 247, 251,
  256, 260
Terry, Ralph.............................. 26
Throneberry, Marv 34
Tiant, Luis 230
Todd, Jim......................... 225, 230
Tolan, Bobby 144, 149, 152
Torrez, Mike..................... 241, 251
Tovar, Cesar 85, 228
Trillo, Manny... 174, 179, 196, 203,
  225
Turner, Ted 31
Uhlaender, Ted 85
Velez, Otto...................... 191–93
Virdon, Bill............................. 193
Voss, Bill.......................... 124–25
Walker, Dr. Harry.................... 179
Washington, Claudell 204, 223–25,
  227, 228, 231, 241, 245, 248
Washington, Herb... 197–200, 210–
  11, 227, 240
Weaver, Earl........................... 172

Index

Webster, Ramon 45, 73
White, Roy 253
Williams, Billy 225–27, 230–31, 248
Williams, Dick 101, 103–4, 110–11, 113, 119, 120, 121, 125–26, 129–31, 133, 134, 145–46, 149–50, 152–53, 157, 161, 164, 171, 175–76, 179–82, 187–94, 203, 248
Williams, Earl 57, 168, 251
Winkles, Bobby 252
Wynn, Jim 209–11
Yastrzemski, Carl 82
Yawkey, Tom 244
Zachary, Chris 132

www.ingramcontent.com/pod-product-compliance
Lightning Source LLC
Chambersburg PA
CBHW032037150426
43194CB00006B/322